Religion
on the
International
News
Agenda

Religion on the International *News* Agenda

Edited by Mark Silk

THE PEW PROGRAM ON RELIGION AND THE NEWS MEDIA

THE LEONARD E. GREENBERG CENTER
FOR THE STUDY OF RELIGION IN PUBLIC LIFE

TRINITY COLLEGE

HARTFORD, CONNECTICUT

2000

Contents

The opinions expressed in this publication are those of the authors and do not necessarily reflect the views of the Pew Charitable Trusts.

120202

Contributors

SAÏD AMIR ARJOMAND is Professor of Sociology at the State University of New York at Stony Brook. He serves as editor of International Sociology, the journal of the International Sociological Association, and is President of the International Association for the Study of Persian-speaking Societies. His books include *The Shadow of God and the Hidden Imam: Religion, Political Order, and Societal Change in Shi'Ite Iran from the Beginning to 1890* and *The Turban for the Crown: The Islamic Revolution in Iran*. He is currently working on a constitutional history of the Islamic Middle East. Phone: (631) 632-7746. E-mail: sarjoman@notes.cc.sunysb.edu.

EILEEN BARKER is Professor of Sociology with Special Reference to the Study of Religion at the London School of Economics. Her more than 170 publications include *The Making of a Moonie: Brainwashing or Choice?* and *New Religious Movements: A Practical Introduction*. In 1988, with the support of the British Government and mainstream religions, she founded INFORM, a non-profit organization that provides information which is as objective and up-to-date as possible about new religious movements. In 1999 she was made an Officer of the Order of the British Empire. Phone: +44 (0) 20-7955-7289. E-mail: E.Barker@LSE.ac.uk.

N. J. DEMERATH III is Professor of Sociology at the University of Massachusetts, Amherst, immediate past President of the Society for the Scientific Study of Religion, and Council Member of the International Society for the Sociology of Religion. A long-time student of religion, his dozen books reflect a recent focus on religion and politics, both at home (*A Bridging of Faiths: Religion and Politics in a New England City*) and abroad (*Crossing the Gods: World Religions and Worldly Politics*). Phone: (413) 545-4068. E-mail demerath@soc.umass.edu.

ROSALIND I. J. HACKETT is Professor of Religious Studies at the University of Tennessee, Knoxville. She is on leave for the 2000-2001 academic year at Harvard University, where she is a Liberal Arts Fellow in Law and Religion at Harvard Law School and a Senior Fellow at the Center for the Study of World Religions. Widely published in the area of African religions and new religious movements, she is currently focusing her research on the implications of the expansion of the media sector in Africa for issues of religious freedom and conflict. She recently co-edited *Religious Persecution as a*

U.S. Policy Issue and is author of the forthcoming *Nigeria: Religion in the Balance*. In August 2000 she was elected Vice President of the International Association for the History of Religions. Phone: (617) 493-4077 (2000-2001); (865) 974-2466. E-mail: rhackett@utk.edu.

ROBERT W. HEFNER is Professor of Anthropology at Boston University and Associate Director at the Institute for the Study of Economic Culture, where he directs the Program in Democracy and Civic Culture. He writes extensively on religion and politics in Southeast Asia, with special focus on Indonesia and Malaysia. His books include *Civil Islam: Muslims and Democratization in Indonesia*, *The Political Economy of Mountain Java*, and *Hindu Javanese: Tengger Tradition and Islam*. During 1998-2000 he directed a Ford Foundation project on the politics of citizenship and ethno-religious pluralism in Malaysia, Singapore, and Indonesia. Phone: (617) 353-2194. E-mail: rhefner@bu.edu.

DANIEL H. LEVINE is Professor of Political Science and Chair of the Department of Political Science at the University of Michigan. He has published extensively on religion and politics in Latin America. His books include *Religion and Politics in Latin America*, *Popular Voices in Latin American Catholicism*, and *Constructing Culture and Power in Latin America*. He served on the Board of Editors of the *Encyclopedia of Politics and Religion*. Phone: (734) 763-3080. E-mail: dhldylan@umich.edu.

MARK SILK is director of the Leonard E. Greenberg Center for the Study of Religion in Public Life and Associate Professor of Religion in Public Life at Trinity College, Hartford. From 1987 to 1996 he was a staff writer, editorial writer, and columnist at the *Atlanta Journal-Constitution*. He edits *Religion in the News*, a review of news coverage of religion, and is the author of *Spiritual Politics: Religion and America Since World War II* and *Unsecular Media: Making News of Religion in America*. He is the editor of *Religion and American Politics: The 2000 Election in Context*. Phone: (860) 297-2352. E-mail: mark.silk@trincoll.edu.

ARTHUR WALDRON is Lauder Professor of International Relations at the University of Pennsylvania and Director of Asian Studies at the American Enterprise Institute. One of America's leading students of Asian politics and culture, he is the author of *The Great Wall of China*, *How the Peace was Lost*, and *From War to Nationalism: China's Turning Point, 1924-1925*. He also contributes frequently to scholarly journals and general circulation periodicals. Phone: (215) 898-6565. E-mail: AWALDRON2@aol.com.

Introduction

Mark Silk

During the Millennium World Peace Summit of Religious and Spiritual Leaders in New York in August 2000, a Zoroastrian priest told Gustav Niebuhr of the *New York Times* that he hoped the gathering would "suppress violence and terrorism that is going on in the name of religion." At the turn of the millennium there is, indeed, little question that religion—or, if one wants to be nice about it, the *name* of religion—has become increasingly associated with conflict around the globe. From Kosovo to Khartoum, from Jerusalem to Jakarta, the struggle for power and pelf both within and between countries can often now be cast in religious terms.

But it is not only as an occasion for violence and terrorism that religion has grown more consequential around the globe. Since the end of the cold war, ethnic and national identity have, at times for the better, taken on a pronounced religious character. In the context of a declining reliance on the power of secular governments to galvanize societies and solve social problems, religions and religiously affiliated institutions have begun to look like plausible candidates to step into the breach. And in some parts of the world, religious belief and practice appear to be on the rise.

All this has undermined the conviction that religion is a declining force in human affairs. The variously understood theory of secularization—whereby Western social thought tended to consider religious decline as an intrinsic dimension of modernization—has had some pretty rough sledding over the past couple of decades. Nor is it merely that religion is proving to be a tougher foe of modernization than anticipated. As Saïd Arjomand points out in this volume, the remarkable revival of Islam in the latter part of the 20th century has been in large measure a product of the very course of advancing literacy, technological development, and globalization that is the very essence of modernization today.

Yet it would be a mistake to conclude that the idea of secularization is simply wrong. Rather, it makes more sense to think, as N. J. Demerath does, in terms of ongoing processes of secularization *and* sacralization, of religion advancing and retreating as part of the normal course of social change. Indeed, there are many ways and many reasons that religious forces advance and retreat in a society, and many roles for religion to play.

In *The Spirit of the Laws* (1748), Montesquieu argued that, in any society, religion ought to make up for deficiencies in the secular order of things, and vice versa: "As religion and the civil laws should aim principally to make good citizens of men, one sees that when either of these departs from this end, the other should aim more toward it." Observing the United States with a Montesquieuian eye a century later, Tocqueville saw religion in Jacksonian America as in fact counterbalancing the tendency of our egalitarian democracy to lead its members into selfishness and an inordinate love of material pleasure. "The great advantage of religions," he wrote, "is to inspire diametrically contrary urges."

Recognizing religion as offering resources to different societies according to their different needs may be the most useful approach to understanding its varied roles on the international scene today. Assuredly, not all of these resources point in the direction of good citizenship. But in most parts of the world, religion is in a dynamic relationship with what all else is going on in society, and its capacity to step up to the plate or retire from the field depending on the exigencies of the times, is notable. Where religion is pushing against state authority in China, it is called upon to undergird it in India. Where religion is arrayed against civil society in Iran, it is promoting it in Latin America. Where religion is undermining pluralism in Africa, it has advanced it in Indonesia. And across the Former Soviet Bloc, all of the above seems to be happening at once.

The purpose of this volume is primarily to help American journalists—editorial writers as well as foreign editors and correspondents—better grasp the religious dimension of important international news stories, and to signal some areas to keep an eye on as these stories develop in the near future. Limits of time and resources prevented coverage of the entire waterfront. The religious aspects of conflicts in Northern Ireland and between Israel and her neighbors, to name just two very well known flashpoints, are not discussed at all. But an effort has been made to offer a picture comprehensive enough to suggest how religion functions in today's world, even where a specific country or situation is not discussed per se.

Each of our seven contributors is a leading expert in his or her area of specialization; together they reflect a range of disciplinary expertise, from sociology and political science to history and anthropology. The group convened in Hartford in the fall of 1999 for a planning session, and the following April presented initial drafts at a conference attended by some two dozen print and broadcast journalists from around the country. What follows has benefited from the lively discussion that took place at the conference.

This is the second volume in a series underwritten by the Pew Charitable Trusts through a grant to the Greenberg Center. The first, *Religion and American Politics: The 2000 Election in Context*, has proved useful not only to working journalists but to a wider public of teachers and interested citizens as well. I hope this will do likewise.

In a Minor Key:
Religion, Politics, and the State in India

N. J. Demerath III

The Indian national anthem is set to a non-Western melody that is reasonably accessible to a Western ear—until its very last note. That note emerges in a minor key and fades hauntingly away as Westerners wait in vain for resolution into a major chord. I last heard the anthem in a January 2000 ceremony marking the end of the 50th anniversary of the Indian constitution and republic. Following as it did a deeply moving band and carillon rendition of Mohandas Gandhi's favorite Anglican hymn, "Abide With Me," the anthem returned us once again from the age of the British raj to the continuing drama of the world's largest democracy—a fractious and at times violent drama that also lacks resolution. It is a drama that revolves around religion.

The single most important factor in religion's connection to violence involves its relation to power, politics, and the state. And yet the possible relationships vary widely. In some cases, religion may turn its back on the state as a defiling digression from more important otherworldly concerns. In other cases, religion may be deeply implicated in either a religious state or, as is more common, a state religion, depending upon which is the dominant partner. In still other cases, there may be a tension between religion and the state, as each plays moth to the other's flame. Even where there is a *de jure* or *de facto* separation between the two, each has something to offer and to gain from the other. In pursuing state power or power over the state, religion is drawn ever closer to the high heat of politics. In pursuing religious legitimacy, the state may be singed or consumed by the flames of emotionally contested meanings.

These tensions are virtually universal, and no country exemplifies them more clearly or with higher stakes than India. In this respect, it is useful to begin by showing where India fits into a global classification of how countries relate religion to politics and the state—a classification that, perhaps surprisingly, finds India and the U.S. similarly situated. By way of introduction, then, let us begin with a few words on the United States, and then broaden these to the world at large before finally focusing on India itself.

To many Americans, the very phrase "religion and politics" smacks of something gone wrong. After all, our First Amendment insists on a "separation" of the two, does it not? It does not. On a picky point, the idea of "separation" (as in "wall of separation") comes only in a letter written by Thomas Jefferson to a group of Baptists in 1803, and the pertinent phrase states only that "Congress shall make no law respecting an establishment of religion or prohibiting the free exercise thereof." On a major point, it is one thing to bar religion from state hegemony—which the First Amendment does—and quite another to bar religion from political involvement by precluding religious practitioners, religious leaders, or for that matter religious organizations from running for office or participating in electoral campaigns—which it does not.

In fact, the sole clause pertinent to religion in the unamended Constitution of 1787 states that "no religious test shall ever be required as qualification to any office or public Trust under the United States" (Article VI). Of course, the prohibition also extends by implication to any test for *non*-religion. American politics are replete with religious candidates of virtually every denominational stripe—clergy as well as laity, elected as well as defeated. The only real—if rarely and reluctantly enforced—penalty for American religious organizations that participate in politics is a loss of tax exemption.

There is little doubt that the founders understood politics as a necessary process of airing competing interests and ideologies. By contrast, the state is an apparatus of government within which successful politicians serve as temporary office-holders under the sufferance of the system and its electorate. Opening politics to religion while keeping the state closed involves one of the less remarked upon of the celebrated "checks and balances" in the American constitutional system. Each practice tends to be contingent on the other, much like the relationship between separationism overall and civil religion described earlier. Religion can be active in politics precisely because we are protected from its state hegemony. Conversely, religion need not have a position within the state because it can air its positions politically.

It is true that mixing religion and politics can lead to a kind of cultural warfare. But this is rare except when state power hangs in the political balance. Politics that follows a lawful pattern in the pursuit of well-defined and constitutionally regulated state offices is quite different from a politics of winner-take-all, including the right to re-define the state rather than merely playing a role within it. Similarly, there is a crucial distinction between the state as an enduring, rule-bound apparatus of government that transcends its incumbent officials of the moment versus the state as the momentary and ideologically opportunistic creation of the last conquering politician, i.e. between the state as a long-term end in its own right and the state as a short-term means to more politically particular ends.

Banning religious considerations and religious leaders from politics is simply unrealistic. Moreover, the attempt to do so is apt to backfire. When religion is denied a place at the political table, it is likely to create more problems—either as an outraged victim of a repressive political system or as an unmonitored force operating in the political shadows. In short, a politics that excludes religion is no more defensible than a state that establishes religion.

Today's world contains everything from religious states and state religions to cases where religion lacks either a legal role in politics or cultural standing in the society at large. Basically, countries can be apportioned among four simplified tendencies: 1) religious politics and a religious state; 2) secular politics and a secular state; 3) secular politics and a religious state; and finally 4) religious politics and a secular state.

Religious States and Religious Politics. From both a conceptual point of view and an historical perspective, this would appear the purest of the four cases, and perhaps the most common stereotype of non-Western, non-secular societies around the world. Because religion in one sphere is matched symmetrically by religion in the other, a religious state would seem to go hand in hand with religious politics.

In fact, the combination is more the exception than the rule, and this is because it is so volatile. When a religious state is faced with active religious politics, there is a religious conflict at issue. Under such circumstances, the state's very legitimacy is called into question, and violence may reflect pre-emptive actions of state control as well as the clash among contending religious parties. If there is a single pattern that lends itself to the most widespread religious and cultural violence, it is surely this one. And, alas, while the category is rare, it is hardly non-existent. It describes the legacy of virtually every Latin American country; it also includes the current situations of both Israel and Northern Ireland. In each of the latter, the state is formally or effectively religious, and the politics have followed tragic suit. Israel and Northern Ireland have hosted some of the most deeply rooted and tragic violence of the modern era. This makes it especially important to consider the alternatives.

Secular States and Secular Politics. If the first combination is stereotypically non-Western, this one is commonly associated with the West. In one sense, it represents a realization of the Enlightenment vision through what Bryan Wilson (1966) called the "secularization of public religion" and what Rodney Stark and Laurence Iannaccone (1994) call the "de-sacralization of the state." The secular-state/secular-politics combination is often associated with Western Europe in particular. But it also applies functionally, if not formally, to Anglican England, which may yet follow the lead of Sweden, which disestablished its state Lutheran church in January 2000. It is true that religious movements lurk in the political shadows of all these countries, but their politics rarely take explicit religious form.

Nor does Europe exhaust the secular-secular category. For example, both Turkey and China qualify in letter, if not always in spirit. Turkey has been officially secular since Ataturk's great transformation in the 1920s, though it has recently required military saber rattling to roust Muslims out of politics and out of power. China is clearly a secular state and has secular politics partly by virtue of having no mass politics at all. Here too, however, there have been recent—if somewhat paranoid problems—in keeping religion out of politics, viz. the repression of the Falun Gong.

Clearly, the combination of a secular state and secular politics has some empirical standing, and it is in some measure correctly associated with Western post-enlightenment developments. But the combination in pure form runs the risk of cultural lassitude, if not sterility. Many of the above cases reveal persisting strains toward some form of religion or "sacred" alternative that state administrations seek to dampen, if not drown. While these new religious developments rarely represent major trends, they are also seldom dismissable. So far, then, we have dealt with the two opposing polar combinations: the doubly religious associated with violence and the doubly secular tending toward vacuity.

Religious States and Secular Politics. There are basically three scenarios that combine a religious state and secular politics. The first occurs when state religiousness is an empty symbol rather than a compelling commitment—more an anachronistic form than a contemporary function. In fact, we noted several such countries under the secular-secular rubric, including "Lutheran" Sweden.

If this first model suggests a certain ritualized indifference to religion, a second version involves a far more active and pointed religious presence. Here religion is an important source of state legitimacy, and no alternative religious views are tolerated. Religion is banned from politics precisely because it is so potentially upsetting as an emotionally charged component of the culture at large. Often politics of any real substance is frowned upon, and religious grievances against the state are suppressed. These are theocracies represented by some traditionally Catholic Latin American states as well as a number of Islamic hegemonies in the Middle East. It also applies to several countries in Southeast Asia such as Buddhist Thailand. Here the state controls the political world very tightly and embraces religion more to co-opt it than to submit to it.

In some ways these first two models of religious states with secular politics are opposites of each other. The first represents religious tokenism in the midst of apathy, while the second reveals an imposed religious order to quell potential religious disorder. Meanwhile, a third qualifies as a perverse variant on the second. This involves states that carefully construct their own religion to frustrate the political mobilization of a genuine religious alternative. Until very recently, Indonesia offered a case in point. Here the state created *pancasila* as an imposed civil religion seeking to bind syncretistically the loyalties of Christians, Hindus, Buddhists, and animists—as well as the 85 percent of the population who are formally Muslims. Under former President Suharto, strict electoral rules made it virtually impossible for any one religious group to rise up against the regime, and the state's administrative apparatus also functioned as a controlling political structure (*golkar*). In all of this, the object was to stifle the development of the so-called "Islamic fundamentalists," some of whose actual agendas were more secular than religious and ultimately led to Suharto's overthrow.

Thus, the combination of a religious state with secular politics makes for even stranger bedfellows than politics alone. All three of its scenarios are somewhat procrustean, and the latter two share a sense of unstable vulnerability as a temporary way-station for cases caught in transition between the other three basic combinations.

Secular States and Religious Politics. Despite my earlier comments, many may regard this as another unlikely combination. If a society is able to sustain a government that is basically secular, isn't this because there is too little religious action to animate its politics significantly? Put oppositely, when any society's politics become religiously infected, how can its state structures fail to catch the virus?

Both questions are reasonable, but once again, the logic behind a secularly neutral state with a free-ranging religious polity is that each complements and constrains the other. There need be no limits to the free exercise of religion in politics as long as there is a strict prohibition of any religious establishment within the state. Politicians, as politicians, may campaign on—and even vote—their religious consciences; nor is there anything to prevent them from bowing to the bidding of their religious organizations. But state officials and state administrations have a different responsibility. They must remain formally and functionally neutral, and not only in the pluralistic fray between religions but also in the larger struggle between religion, on the one hand, and secularism, on the other. The overall result should be a contested but vital politics framed by an equitable state that rises above the fray to guarantee fairness to all. In the final analysis, a religion's capital is best optimized when it is not a capital religion.

This at least describes the constitutional theory and founding enthusiasm behind two countries that constitute the world's largest and oldest democracies respectively; namely, the India and U.S. Unfortunately, neither the theory nor the practice is fully appreciated in either country.

On December 6, 1992 in the north-central Indian city of Ayodhya, followers of the Hindu nationalist Bharatiya Janata Party (BJP) broke out of a demonstration protesting the existence of a mosque on the site of what many Hindus considered the exact birthplace of their revered god, Rama. The mob razed the structure stone by stone, leaving only a pile of rubble at day's end. The incident triggered another round in the communal religious violence that has become a tragic trademark of India. The resulting riots in cities like Bombay ultimately left some 1,700 dead and almost 6,000 injured.

Why? How can one account for such civil strife? A determined demographic determinist might argue that size and density alone are the problem. After all, India has three times the population of the U.S. in only one-third the area; it now claims roughly one-sixth of the world's population and not long into the 21st century will overtake China as the globe's most populous country. However, China's own relatively low level of civil strife rebuts a strict demographic explanation. Clearly there are other cancers gnawing at India's simultaneously new and ancient corpus.

Describing India quickly puts one in mind of India's own cliché concerning the blind men describing an elephant as each touched only a part—though an irrepressible colleague once responded, "But some of us are on the ball." India's visitors often find the country a bewildering conundrum—both a stimulant and a depressant, both sensuously seductive in its sounds, tastes, and colors, and gloweringly formidable in its poverty, pollution, and alien uniqueness of manners and custom. There is no denying the splendor, the violence, or the singularity. Indeed, these sometimes coalesce in a single image—for example, the bright vermilion sari worn by a woman picking through the trash on one of Calcutta's mountains of garbage with her naked children searching nearby.

India is singular in so many ways, including in its temporal status as the only major nation that counts time on the half-hour relative to the rest of the world. Until just a few years ago, India was also the one remaining great civilization that had not yet been invaded by McDonald's. Alas, that distinction has recently faded: in India's transition from a closed socialism to a more open capitalism, the Golden Arches have arrived with lamb-based "Maharajah Macs" designed to offend neither the cow-revering Hindus nor the pork-abstaining Muslims.

But how does one begin to portray so vast a civilization with a 4,000-year memory? India has spawned two of the world's great religious traditions (Hinduism and Buddhism), generated several other important religious communities (the Jains and the Sikhs), and played reluctant host to two other major world religions (Islam and Christianity)? India spreads down from the world's highest mountains in the Himalayan north across fertile plains, arid deserts, and rocky hills to the Arabian Sea on the West, the Bay of Bengal on the East, and at its southernmost point to the Gulf of Mannar, across which lies the small but no less conflicted island nation of Sri Lanka.

India was more a culture quilt than a tightly bound nation for most of its history. In one sense it was ripe to be conquered because it was already divided, and its political unity is the bittersweet legacy of two outside incursions: first, a dynasty of Muslim "moghul" emperors who ruled in the north from the early 16th to the late 19th century; and second, the British East India Company and then the British government itself that ruled until 1947. Even independence combined the bitter with the sweet. Under the leadership of the great Gandhi, this was the climactic achievement of one of the greatest social movements in world history and the fulfillment of a democratic dream.

But it also involved a nightmare of Hindu-Muslim violence. Negotiations for independence finally yielded not one but two new nations—the gigantic, poly-cultural but dominantly Hindu India on the one hand, and on the other, the Muslim state of a combined West and East Pakistan (the latter becoming still a third independent state of Bangladesh in 1971). When independence was originally realized in August 1947, Hindus and Muslims alike were stranded away from their new homelands and began desperate migrations across the borders with grotesque consequences. As many as half a million people were slaughtered in one of the world's most tragic episodes of religious conflict. (Collins and Lapierre, 1975)

And yet, in the 30 years or so that followed, India's government shimmered as a political exemplar. Beginning in the 1980s, however, the country's past began to catch up with its present, and its religious conflicts began to infect its politics once again. By 1980, the proudly independent democracy of India was in the hands of a second generation of leaders. The great Jawaharlal Nehru had died, and the mantle of party and national leadership had fallen to his daughter, Indira Gandhi (no relation to Mohandas). But troubles once deferred had begun to resurface. There was still no resolution of the dispute over Jammu-Kashmir—officially part of India but claimed by Pakistan because of its Muslim majority. Just as today, lives continued to be sacrificed in the battle between the Indian Army and Muslim insurgents allegedly supported by the Pakistani government. And this was only one of several areas with movements pressing for secession. Virtually every corner of the society was being nibbled at from the inside.

Not least of these was another area bordering Pakistan southwest of Kashmir. This was the Punjab—the area of greatest Sikh concentration— where a group of Sikh insurgents led by Sant ("priest") Jarnail Singh Bhindranwale pressed for an independent nation. Mrs. Gandhi, the Prime Minister, first sought to head off the impasse by befriending Bhindranwale so as to better reason with him. But later she sent troops into the sacred Sikh "Golden Temple" of Amritsar, where in 1984 tragedy leapt from the barrels of military guns. Some 500 Sikh militants were killed, including Bhindranwale himself. In light of her earlier overtures to the Sikhs, this was seen as an act of betrayal, and Indira Gandhi was assassinated by her own Sikh bodyguards later that same year.

If the killing of Bhindranwale illustrates what can happen when a religious moth gets too close to the political flame, the assassinations of the Mohandas and Indira Gandhi show that the reverse scenario can lead to the same sad denouement as political moths are consumed by religious flames. Mrs. Gandhi was ultimately succeeded as Prime Minister by her son, Rajiv Gandhi, an engineer and commercial pilot who never shared the family's political enthusiasm or experience. Alas, he too was assassinated—in 1991 by Tamil separatists in southeast India. Still another moth and another flame.

Meanwhile, consider a very different case that had already been working its way towards a different national convulsion. In 1975, in the central India district of Indore, a relatively prosperous Muslim man expelled his first of two wives following 43 years of marriage and five children. In 1978, the wife— Shah Bono—filed a criminal complaint asking for the equivalent of $38 per month maintenance from her husband's annual income of some $4,600. At this point, the husband availed himself of a special provision in Indian law enacted in 1950 when the 12 percent Islamic minority was allowed to conduct matters of birth, marriage, and death under a separate "Muslim Personal Law" controlled by mullahs. Accordingly, Mr. Bono effected a "triple divorce" by simply repeating "I divorce you" three times. Although he had paid some $15/month for the two years following separation, he argued that this ended his liabilities—according to Muslim law (*shari`ah*).

Normally a Muslim wife would relent, but not Shah Bono. To simplify a complicated chain of legal actions and appeals, she pursued her case to the Indian Supreme Court, insisting on her rights not just as a Muslim but as an Indian citizen. In 1985, the Court held that the husband was indeed liable according to an Indian criminal statute concerning acts that may produce vagrancy, and that his wife's Muslim treatment had involved misinterpretations of both *shari`ah* and the Koran. Accordingly, Shah Bono was awarded a monthly allowance of roughly $14. Not surprisingly, the traditional Islamic community was furious, and the mullahs quickly began to mobilize politically. While there was some lower court precedent for the decision itself, Muslim traditionalists were especially affronted by the impertinence of a Hindu Court arrogantly instructing mullahs on how to interpret the Koran instead of consulting them.

Welcome to the prime ministership, Mr. Gandhi. Over the next several years, the inexperienced Rajiv took two actions that mollified the mullahs. First, he spearheaded a bill through parliament that effectively reversed the Supreme Court action and restored Muslim authority in matters of divorce. Second, he buckled under another wave of traditional Muslim pressure and banned Salmon Rushdie's novel, *The Satanic Verses*.

As much as both of these actions met with Muslim approval, they were greeted with special scorn and contempt from traditional Hindus who saw this as just more evidence of the bogus secular neutrality of the ruling Congress Party and the Indian state. Far from being neutral, they were actually pro-Islamic. Rajiv became quickly aware of his political miscalculation. There was one particular action that would help him make amends with the Hindu right. This involved the contested mosque and Rama's birthplace in Ayodhya. Such disputes over jointly claimed sacred sites are not rare in India, and this one dated back to the late 1880s. In 1947 Hindus broke into the mosque, placed an idol of Rama there, and claimed a miracle. At that point, the local judge locked up the mosque, idol and all. While a Brahmin was allowed in to conduct periodic *puja* for the idol; all others—Hindus and Muslims alike—were denied access.

This continued to rankle many Hindus, who saw the government's concession to the Muslims following the Shah Bono case as a final straw on the camel's sagging back. Ayodyah became a *cause célèbre* for "Hindutva"—a term coined in 1923 by the scholar-demagogue, V. Savarkar, that now refers to all right-wing Hindu nationalist groups, ranging from the R.S.S. youth brigade and the vitriolic Shiv Sena to the BJP Political Party. Rama had become even more popular as a result of the television series depicting his exploits. Under pressure from his fellow Hindus—and, it is rumored, Rajiv Gandhi himself— a local judge ordered the gates to the mosque re-opened in 1986. Rajiv himself participated in the ceremonies.

The BJP continued to key its political campaign to Rama and Ayodyah. It launched a massive caravan across northern India featuring the party leader in a jeep decorated as Rama's chariot. The campaign climaxed with the massive rally in Ayodhya that dissolved into day-long destruction mosque described earlier.

What has happened since 1992? Despite initial pledges and a Supreme Court order to rebuild the mosque and produce a joint Hindu-Muslim site, the matter has become entangled in both political and bureaucratic underbrush. The Supreme Court has been dilatory, perhaps deliberately, in hearing an appeal of the bill that overturned its Shah Bono decision. However, there is some indication that lower courts are increasingly following the Supreme Court's example anyway in many such cases. There is even some hope that the courts can provide what Parliament cannot; namely, a *de facto*, if not *de jure*, Uniform Civil Code that applies to Indians of all faiths. To the extent that such a code requires a Solomonic compromise between Hindu and Muslim codes that are themselves internally contested, it is a political impossibility. But such a code may have a chance if it is interpreted less grandiosely as simply a set of minimum national standards to which all citizens are held and entitled but beyond which they may freely invoke religious traditions and rituals.

As Muslim-Hindu conflicts continue to simmer and erupt throughout India, some suggest that there are mollifying developments at work within the Muslim community. Here as elsewhere in the Muslim world, women are increasingly mobilized for change. And a new generation of educated Muslims has filled the leadership void left by partition a half-century ago. Many seek to avoid the trap of tit-for-tat violence while seeking new accommodation with older and more aggressive Muslim and Hindu leaders.

And yet the march of Hindutva has quickened. It is directed as much at secular reformers as at Muslims and adherents of other faiths. The BJP looms ever larger on the national political scene. A series of corruption scandals exacted a major toll on the long dominant Congress Party and left many wondering who would succeed leaders now in their 70s and 80s. Despite the efforts of Rajiv's Italian widow, Sonia, and hopes resting upon their daughter, Priyantka, there is a broad sense of what Ramesh Thakur (1993) has called "regime decay." Two of my respondents provided neatly parallel accounts of how the two parties have cooperated to keep religion roiling on the political stove.

On one side: "Sure, the BJP is trying to normalize itself as a mass party, not just a religious party. But Congress won't let us de-emphasize religion. They keep throwing it in our face." And on the other: "The BJP really hijacked most of Congress's standard political and economic agenda, and the only card left for Congress to play involved religion and the betrayal of secularism."

When India obtained independence in 1947 it took three years to carefully develop a constitution that reflected a number of Western models, especially that of the U.S. However, a growing complaint within India today is that its independence leaders were too quick to apply Western secular forms of government to an Eastern cultural reality that required its own unique state response. There is now a strong strain away from the combination of a secular state and religious politics towards that most volatile alternative of a religious state with religious politics, which I described earlier.

The argument holds that a secular state may work well enough in a country like the U.S., but that it is discordant within an Indian society that remains so intransigently non-secular at its core (Madan 1992, 1998). Indeed, the very imposition of Western secularism has served perversely to fan the flames of religious extremism by forcing religious advocates to adopt aggressive measures to make their case—measures that even include communal violence. Some go so far as to suggest that India is not just a deeply religious country but a fundamentally Hindu society that can only be led by a Hindu government. As Hinduism finds its natural expression in state control, it will revert back to its natural historical tolerance of the minority religions in its domain.

And yet this is only one reading of the Indian case. By no means have all Indian intellectuals thrown in the secular towel. Many continue to resist both religious and anti-religious models of the state in favor of a more neutral or "a-religious" reading of the Indian Constitution. From this perspective, the cause of communal violence is not that the state is too secular but rather that it is not secular enough. Not that the state should use its influence to curb or end religion, but rather, it should be impartial among contesting religious groups and concerning the larger question of religion versus non-religion as a cultural desideratum. From the very outset, religion was implicated in the Indian constitution and the government it conceived (Smith, 1963). From the beginning, there were controversial religious actions, including a state exemption for Muslims to follow Islamic rather than national laws in personal matters, as well as liberal reforms of Hinduism concerning such matters as temple administration and a continuation of the British "reservations policy" designed to provide a form of occupational affirmative action for *dalits* ("untouchables").

These exceptions in secular state policy have festered over the years. From a neutral vantage point, religious personal obligations are fine as long as they do not contradict the minimal rights and responsibilities of the citizenry at large. Some argue that rather than use religious status as a basis for reserving jobs, affirmative action should be based on more general socio-economic disadvantage, and that it is educational access that should be reserved, not actual employment. Nothing vexes high-caste Brahmins more than jobs going to middle-class and quite well educated untouchables; this is known widely as the "creamy layer problem."

In any event, it is clear that India's chronic "communal violence" (Hindus vs. Muslims in Ayodyah, Bombay, and Kashmir; Hindus vs. Christians in Gujarat and Orissa; Sikhs vs. Hindus in the Punjab; southern Tamil rebels mobilizing against Buddhists in Sri Lanka) reflects the tendency of state leaders and state structures to become embroiled in religious conflicts. One political figure put it this way: "Freedom of religion also means freedom from religion. There is now too much religiosity and too little real religion."

As concessions made to one group require balancing concessions to its rival, constructing state policy has come to resemble shortening a chair one leg at a time: The results are never quite even, and the seat of power becomes increasingly unstable. The assassinations of both Indira and Rajiv Gandhi offer tragic reminders of the possible consequences. Clearly, national pride in an independent democratic state has eroded somewhat over the past half-century. As to India's current titular President—an old "Congress man" and the first *dalit* to be appointed to such high office—commented, "We have to consider whether it is the Constitution that has failed us, or us the Constitution."

In one sense, there has been a secularization of the very concept of the secular state, as an ideal that has lost its luster. But semantics here can be confusing. In 1976, almost as a last gasp, India's independence leaders amended the Constitution to refer to a "Secular Democratic Republic." This was widely interpreted to signify "secularism" as official state policy. And yet there are subtle differences between "secularism" as an explicit ideology of non-religion, "secularity" as a structural attribute of neutrality with respect to religion, and "secularization" as a historical process that partly operates in dialectical tandem with the countervailing forces of "sacralization." The ideology of secularism may characterize politicians but rarely an entire society. Secularity may well apply—and may apply well—to the state but again not to whole societies. Secularization characterizes all societies in all of their cultural dimensions, religious and non-religious.

But as one scholarly pundit put it: "We have been badly served by the Constitution's wrong choice of words. State secularism is difficult to defend because it seems like a reproach to every religion. One wonders whether the choice of secularism as opposed to more neutral secularity didn't reflect a mischievous compromise at the last moment."

Meanwhile, the distinguished Indian historian, Romila Thapar (1993) takes keen exception to the new "revisionist" portrayal of Hinduism as a once monolithic and sweetly beneficent religion. This image qualifies as another of what Benedict Anderson (1983) has called "imagined communities"—though in an important sense every community that coheres requires just such imagination. Historically, Hinduism has long been a pluralistic patchwork of diverse devotees and divided castes. In fact, the internal variation among Sikhs, Muslims, and most especially Hindus is a major reason why the country has not been drawn into one massive communal war.

Hinduism has exhibited both tolerance and intolerance. Lacking an activist proselytizing impulse or the priestly leadership and organizational coherence required for such a task, Hinduism is the one major world religion that has not sought to conquer other religions, cultures, and countries. Insofar as Hinduism can be found in such other places as Nepal, Indonesia's Bali, and indeed the U.S., this has been more a function of migration than conquest.

On the other hand, precisely because Hinduism lacks such a sociological core, some of its adherents are vulnerable to the appeal of an unceasing array of religious gurus and political mobilizers who provide more immediate gratifications. A number of my informants described friends in the leadership of Hindutva and the BJP as basically secular men with a mission that is more political than religious. While it would be too strong to suggest that Hinduism has been hijacked by Hindutva, this is a possibility that always lurks when power is at stake, especially when an entire national governmental seems to hang in the balance as the once dominant Congress Party seems to be giving way to a conflicted array of contesting alternatives.

In 1993 I departed from India on the first anniversary of the destruction of the Ayodhya mosque. As my taxi drove to the airport we went under graffiti on an overpass that read, "Forget the BJP. The People's Movement for Secularism." Since then, however, the BJP has been anything but forgotten. In 1996 it finally attained sufficient parliamentary power to puts its own prime minister in office at the head of a somewhat precarious multi-party coalition on the political right. The coalition lasted less than three years but before it buckled, it escalated Hindu-Muslim conflict to a larger plane with far greater stakes. The government conducted nuclear-weapons tests that sent a shiver around the world and a glove across the face of its neighboring Muslim rival, Pakistan, which has a fugitive nuclear capacity of its own. As more than one observer has noted, the world now has both Hindu and Muslim nuclear weapons in addition to the long-standing Christian and atheist storehouses in the West and Russia. This is hardly a comforting religious parity.

In fact, the West has recently been drawn into India's religious conflict in yet another way. Several Indian states—notably Orissa and Mohandas Gandhi's own Gujurat—have been the sites of Hindu attacks on poor Christian churches and communities. Insofar as Christians have proselytized disproportionately among the "untouchables" of the scheduled castes, some Hindus see them as interfering with the cosmic social order of reincarnation. Nor has the BJP government been quick to condemn the attacks.

And so the time-honored struggle goes on in this timeless society. India shares with many other countries a contested religious diversity whose short-run conflicts carry enormous long-range consequences. Disputed sacred turf can become a min(d)field with explosive potential. Many more lives are sure to be lost in the name of religions intended to be life-enriching. Still, as one older sage assured me, "Of course, India will survive. But then India has never been a nation so much as a civilization. That is hard for Westerners to understand, but we know very well what it means."

Most recently I left India on January 30th, 2000, the "Martyr's Day" anniversary of Mohandas Gandhi's assassination by a Hindu extremist in 1948. Minutes before writing this, I learned that an Indian government official had taken it upon himself to censor a *Time* magazine interview with the still-living brother of the executed assassin, Nathuram Godse, on the grounds that the material was too inflammatory. It seemed ironic that an Indian action against an alleged excess of Western media coverage occurred on the very day I was to write about the perceived paucity of such coverage.

The paucity is easily demonstrated. Over a two-week period, I counted some 24 stories bearing on religion that appeared in two or more of India's English-language daily newspapers. Only two of these surfaced in the *New York Times*, the AP, or Reuters, not to mention our regional or local papers. These concerned the trek of the 14-year-old Buddhist Karmapa Llama from Chinese Tibet to India and the continuing Indian-Pakistani dispute over dominantly Muslim Kashmir. The Indian press has long referred to the latter as "the proxy war" because of the involvement of Pakistan's alleged proxy guerillas. Recently, however, the press has used the phrase "Kargil war" to honor India's recent triumph in re-taking Kargil Hill from the insurgents—an event that was re-enacted in a great outdoor sound-and-light theatrical celebration produced and directed by a husband and wife who are both Muslims. Meanwhile, three other stories also appeared concerning trade talks with India, the India-Pakistan nuclear facedown, and a cabdriver in New York who is regarded as a philanthropist in his home village in India.

Of course, covering India is a bit like covering all humanity. And even reasonably complete reporting of developments in Indian religion is unrealistic in a country where religion and caste considerations seem to pervade everything from dramas of personal life to tensions of electoral politics and foreign policy. To be fair, the Indian press does even worse in covering the U.S.

As a rule of thumb, any nation's press coverage of another seems to decline with every social distinction interposed, whether these concern differences of regional location, political power, economic interest, language, ethnicity, or religion. From the standpoint of the U.S., India is alien on all counts and out of mind is often out of sight. A few newspapers and news agencies have moved reporters into India since the 1999 nuclear escalation with Pakistan, but most

Western journalists still arrive on a newsworthy scene from home bases in Hong Kong, Singapore, or Istanbul.

And yet when I talked with Indians who had spent time in the West dependent upon Western media reports on their home country, they were concerned with the quality of Western coverage as well as its quantity. One affirmed the waggish comment of a recent American ambassador who reversed the old cliché to state, "Good news is no news," from the Western media's perspective. There is considerable sensitivity that only bad news makes it to the West, with the result that India is portrayed as a nation on a hair-trigger whose various religious communities are constantly and totally at each other's throats.

Several were concerned with an exoticization of India that perpetuates old stereotypes. One recalled being approached for an interview about a bizarre incident concerning the murder of a lower-caste wife by her cooperating parents and in-laws. When he asked the reporter why he was being asked again about this story in view of the many other stories possible, he was told, "Because our readers really like that kind of stuff about India." I talked to one Western radio reporter who had not only talked the talk in Kashmir but courageously walked the walk with Indian troops under fire. When I hesitantly suggested that it might be better if he were asked for fewer heroics and more library work, he readily agreed.

Of course, news by definition involves the exception rather than the rule—and none of these complaints will come as news to journalists. But my Indian respondents lamented a consistent failure to place news in a day-to-day context while monitoring emerging realities. The very desperation of the Hindutva right suggests that religion and caste are changing with greater urbanization, education, and economic development (Gupta, 1992). According to one respondent, "Westerners all seem to key on aspects of India that are fading pretty fast. Caste and caste politics aren't nearly what they used to be. Traditional religious forces are fighting desperate rearguard actions with desperate measures. There really is a new India emerging, for better or for worse." For example, India's borders are suddenly open externally even as they are contested internally, and the very notion of nationhood is under renegotiation (Khilnani, 1997).

In 1981, D. R. Mankekar, distinguished editor of *The Times of India*—a paper now undergoing "Rupertization"—wrote a book detailing many of the foregoing complaints and calling for improvements in global media coverage, including a code of conduct, an international media council, and the right of national reply under the auspices of the U.N. (Mankekar, 1981). If any of these proposals have been implemented on paper, I have my doubts about their effectiveness in practice. After all, journalism is not only a cultural producer but a cultural product. From the standpoint of the West, nations like India will continue for a while to be heard not only in a minor key but in minor notes.

Issues to Keep an Eye on

Constitutional change. A new BJP-appointed committee is meeting now to open the Pandora's box of constitutional change. Any recommended changes affecting religion and the secularly neutral state would be volatile.

Caste violence. There has been a rise in caste violence as traditional caste rankings are subjected to new scrutiny and begin to give way to resentment and reshuffling at every level. Tribal groups, untouchables, and once-born caste members are increasingly restive. Brahmins and kshatriyas have festering problems with the extended reservations policy (i.e., affirmative action).

Conflict within the Right. It is important to recognize increasing tension between the Hindu-oriented BJP political party, on the one hand, and the extremist Hindutva movement and its various elements (Shiv Sena, RSS, etc.), on the other. As the BJP makes its move towards a mass party, it will have to soft-peddle its original religious militancy, and this will have abrasive consequences.

Political leadership. Who will surface as the next generation of political leaders in India? Both Congress Party and the BJP are dominated by geriatric veterans of the old political wars, and smaller state-based parties have begun to make their moves, often behind younger and more charismatic leaders. Congress is especially interesting under the titular leadership of Sonia Gandhi (the Italian widow of the assassinated Rajiv) and her somewhat uppity daughter, Priyantka.

Kashmir. Dominantly Hindu India and almost exclusively Muslim Pakistan have been stalemated for more than 50 years over the formally Indian state of dominantly Muslim "Jammu-Kashmir." Recently the stakes have risen dramatically with nuclear weapons and political instability on both sides. Armed Muslim insurgents are at work from inside the area with outside help as the Indian military tries to keep the lid on with a strong hand. There are few local conflicts today that are resolvable in local terms (e.g., South Africa, Guatemala, Rwanda). This is surely not one of them.

References

Anderson, Benedict. 1983. *Imagined Communities*. London Routledge, Chapman and Hall.

Collins, Larry, and Dominique Lapierre. 1975. *Freedom at Midnight*. New York: Simon and Schuster.

Demerath, N.J. lll. and Rhys H. Williams. 1992. *A Bridging of Faiths: Religion and Politics in a New England City*. Princeton: Princeton University Press.

Gupta, Dipankar. 1992. "Continuous Hierarchies and Discrete Castes." In D. Gupta, ed. *Social Stratification*, Delhi: Oxford U. Press, pp, 110-142.

Khilnani, Sunil. 1997. *The Idea of India*. Delhi: Oxford University Press.

Madan, T.N.. 1992. "Secularism In Its Place," reprinted in T.N Madan, ed., *Religion in India*. Delhi: Oxford University Press.

_____. 1998. *Modern Myths, Locked Minds*. Delhi: Oxford University Press.

Mankekar, D.R. 1981. *Whose Freedom? Whose Order? A Plea for a New International Information Order by Third World* [sic]. Delhi: Clarion Books.

Smith, Donald E. 1963. *India as a Secular State*. Princeton: Princeton University Press.

Thakur, Ramesh. 1993. "Ayodhya and the Politics of India's Secularism: A Double-Standards Discourse." *Asian Survey* (July).

Thapar, Romila. 1989. "Imagined and Religious Communities: Ancient History and the Modern Search for a Hindu Identity." *Modern Asian Studies*.

❙❙

Religion and the Chinese State

Arthur Waldron

In the realm of religion, what has followed Mao Zedong's death in 1976 has been a complete surprise. In Mao's China, organized religion was more completely suppressed than anywhere else in 20th-century history (with the possible exceptions of Albania and North Korea). So much was it suppressed that by the end of the Cultural Revolution in the mid-1970s most observers agreed that it was "dead."[1] The most that anyone expected in 1982—when the Communist Party slightly lifted the total ban on religious practice imposed in 1966—was that a few old people might return to the handful of reopened temples and churches (all of which were under strict government control). No one anticipated that China's larger course toward a secular and communist state would be affected.[2]

In fact, religion of every kind took off, from the traditional Chinese folk-Buddhism and folk-Daoism of the masses, to the Islam of the country's west and far west, to the Protestant and Catholic Christianity introduced by missionaries and for that reason considered to be the most dead of all. Young people, party cadres, intellectuals, farmers—many returned to belief and it was party orthodoxy that came into question.

The Chinese State, in the form of the communist regime in Beijing, has yet fully to come to terms with this development, for many reasons (as will be seen) but especially for one on which this essay will focus. This is that the structure and nature of religion in China fundamentally changed between the 1950s, when the Communists first came to power, and the 1980s, when the door to practice was slightly opened. What had been an organized and collective enterprise, and thus one amenable to state control inserted at the top, had, during the sixteen years when even officially sponsored religion was banned, become an individual matter. Because belief was no longer a matter of social conformity, it became more powerful. And the very extensive religious structures that the believers improvised were effectively beyond the reach of the state. Under the totalitarianism of the Cultural Revolution, paradoxically enough, religion was established as a first beachhead of genuine civil society.

In most countries, even unfree countries, the government allows some

---

[1] Tony Lambert, *The Resurrection of the Chinese Church* (Wheaton, Illinois: Harold Shaw, 1994), p. 9.

[2] ibid., pp. 51 ff.

space for religion. It may be governed by concordats or restricted from some activities, but it is otherwise left alone. The same approach would probably work in China. Most religious believers there ask no more. But because China has, in effect, an established religion in the form of communism, the astonishing vigor of the alternative faiths poses a direct threat to governmental authority even today, at a time when the leeway for individual activity is greater than at any time since the early 1950s. Largely because of the way the government understands its own claims to legitimacy, the issues of religion and the state are far more important today than might be imagined.[3]

Christianity is the faith of only a small minority of China's people, although in absolute terms the number of Christians, perhaps in the tens of millions, is impressive and higher than ever before. It differs from native faiths such as Daoism and Confucianism, and from the earlier import Buddhism, both in its mode of introduction to China and also, arguably, in the quality of adherence it demands. But Christianity is nevertheless an index of sorts for religion in China generally. Because its vicissitudes are rather well documented, I will return to it repeatedly in the course of this discussion.

Catholicism, was for better or worse a pillar of the state in Europe from the time of Constantine; it was thus a parallel with Confucianism, which was the official faith of Chinese dynasties until the last emperor abdicated in 1912. After an interregnum of 40 years that saw every other religion flourish in China but no established religion support the state, the People's Republic of China introduced, after 1949, a new faith in the form of communism which gave to those who believed in it the same sort of perspective and certainty that other established religions give their followers.

Today, however, communism as a faith is in tatters, though the state founded upon it continues to exist and to make, in theory at least, the sorts of absolute moral claims that are traditionally the prerogatives of religion. But those claims, which provide the state the moral legitimacy that other regimes derive from elections, find fewer and fewer adherents. For this reason, the problem in China is not "church and state" as we understand it in the United States. Rather it is closer to the "orthodoxy versus heresy" of early modern Europe.

Foreign observers of China are regularly wrong, but few have been more wrong than the 18th-century French *philosophes*, who imagined that country to be a land free of superstition—ruled instead by Confucianism, a humane religion of reason. Their vision was clouded by the need for a foil to the France of their own time, with its established Roman Catholic Church.

Buddhism was then, as it is now, the belief of most of China's population, and anyone who finds relics, saints' altars, and the like off-putting in Catholicism will flee in horror from Buddhism, which, though it is as profound and austere as any religion at its highest levels, is in its popular mani-

---

[3] See Arthur Waldron, "Religious Revivals in Communist China," *Orbis* (Spring 1998), pp. 325-334.

festations a confusing and superstitious array. The *philosophes* simply never mentioned this.

Even Confucianism is perhaps not quite the cult of reason that 18th-century Europe imagined. It can serve state ends, to be sure, but the demands it makes on the individual for faith and loyalty are comparable in their totality to those of Catholicism and greater than those of Buddhism or Daoism. Not surprisingly, then, Confucianism has long been at the top of Chinese communism's list of enemies. The Chinese communist attitude towards religion has deep roots, of course, in European Marxism, "scientific atheism," and the religious policies of Stalin. But it also traces back to the attack on Confucianism of the New Culture Movement of the 1910s that was directed against Yuan Shikai, a former Qing dynasty general then in charge in Beijing who sought to restore monarchical rule. Rather than attack Yuan directly, his opponents took as their target the whole tradition of Chinese civilization from which he sought to derive his legitimacy; they argued that until Confucianism was expunged, China could have no hope.

Tendentious as they were, these attacks were powerful and often expressed brilliantly, and they took a real toll. Confucian values were portrayed as hypocritical or worse. For example, in *Family*, a great bestseller of the 1930s and a bible for alienated youth, Ba Jin [Pa Chin] associates a minor Confucian tract with the grotesquely corrupt and hypocritical patriarch of the family. The free-thinking and progressive son is appalled by the hypocrisy of his grandfather's ostensible loyalty to traditional values:

> That book *Yeh-yeh* [Grandfather] gave me—"On Filial Piety and the Shunning of Lewdness"—was still on the table. I picked it up and skimmed through a few pages. The whole thing is nothing but lessons on how to behave like a slave. It's full of phrases like "The minister who is unwilling to die at his sovereign's command is not loyal; the son who is unwilling to die at his father's command is not filial," and "Of all crimes, lewdness is the worst; of all virtues, filial piety is the best." The more I read, the angrier I became, until I got so mad I ripped the book to pieces. With one less copy of that book in the world, a few less people will be harmed by it.[4]

For Lu Xun [Lu Hsun], arguably China's greatest 20th-century writer, the tradition was worse even than hypocritical. Confucian values, translated into practice, led to positive evil, as he made clear in his famous allegory, *Madman's Diary*:

> Everything requires careful consideration if one is to understand it.

---

[4] Pa Chin, *Family* (Boston: Cheng & Tsui Company, 1992), pp. 85-86.

In ancient times, as I recollect, people often ate human beings, but
I am rather hazy about it. I tried to look it up, but my history has
no chronology, and scrawled all over each page are the words:
"Virtue and Morality." Since I could not sleep anyway, I read
intently half the night, until I began to see words between the lines,
the whole book being filled with the two words—"Eat people.[5]

Powerful condemnations to be sure, but the truth was not so simple.
Whatever its defects may have been in practice, Confucianism is a profound
philosophical and religious system. For traditional China it provided the moral
keel, invisible most of the time, for society and the state, and communism has
been unable to replace it. Why? Because the scholar-official class of traditional China was not simply a rational civil service. The goals and guidelines for
the government were moral and drawn from the classics. Unlike priests, the
scholar-officials married; given China's extended family system, this created
even more of a vested interest than a married priesthood would have created
in the West. And although many scholar-officials were far from pious, there
was still something sacred about the classics and their teachings. Norms were
taught and then absorbed and internalized.

In China, control from the center was impossible. Something had to
restrain those beyond the court's view and that something was the moral vision.
The result was the legend, at least, of the upright official, like Hai Rui of the
Ming, who was willing to die rather than cease his remonstrance of the emper-
or. To be sure, such officials were in practice rare. Rule largely followed legal-
ist prescriptions, not Confucian ones.[6] As Frederick Mote explains, "So for the
two thousand years of post-Ch'in imperial Chinese history, the Chinese state
has in fact lived with and become quite adjusted to the dilemma of *being* something that it could not openly proclaim and defend."[7]

Even if not institutionally expressed, however, Confucianism had a powerful impact on the moral orientation of individuals, both in the mass and in the
elite, and in a way that was clearly religious, in the sense of "binding."
Confucianism, as Michel Masson points out, is not just a matter of utilitarian
calculus. It is not simply a list of moral precepts and injunctions about eti-
quette. It is a faith in a moral reality that governs human life even as it transcends it. It rests on the same quality of assurance and manifests itself in the
same sort of conviction as any more explicitly divine religion. "Faith" is ultimately the issue, as was clear in the career of the great 20th-century philoso-

---

[5] "A Madman's Diary." p. 10, in *Selected Stories of Lu Hsun*, tr. Yang Hsien-yi and Gladys Yang
(Peking: Foreign Languages Press, 1978).

[6] Zhengyuan Fu, *Autocratic Tradition and Chinese Politics* (Cambridge: Cambridge University
Press, 1993).

[7] Frederick W. Mote, *Intellectual Foundations of China* (New York: Knopf, 1971), p. 115.

pher (and Confucian) Fung Yu-lan.[8] Confucianism provided moral direction to the elite, just as popular Buddhism and Daoism (and in some areas, Christianity) provided it to the masses, as Lamaism did in Tibet, and as Islam did in Xinjiang and the west.

Communist beliefs once seemed ready to take over the role these religions had played. In the early years of the People's Republic, the indoctrination of the educated young into communism and the Maoist personality cult was as thorough as anything seen in the USSR and Nazi Germany—states, it should be noted, where religion came under attack precisely because it gave the individual something to anchor other than the party or the leader.

Children growing up in devoutly communist families in China shunned the wonderful folk customs of Chinese New Year as severely as New England Puritans shunned Christmas; and if Puritan children grew up aware of the presence of their God, so did their Chinese counterparts know Mao. One recalls: "At home, 'Mao' had been my first word after 'Mama,' 'Baba' [daddy] and 'Nai Nai' [grandma] for I had been held up to the large framed picture Father had hung over the doorway and instructed in the sound. Later I had learned how to say 'I love Chairman Mao' and 'Long Live Chairman Mao.'"[9]

As long as Mao lived, he directed the power of the state against every other form of faith with a destructive fury that has few historical parallels; nor has this entirely abated even today, a quarter-century after his death. At the same time, Maoist beliefs were thoroughly spread throughout Chinese society. If social engineering of religion ever received a full test, this was it. But the result was neither the triumph of Maoism nor the elimination of the alternatives. At best, the Chinese Communists devastated their competition and created a vast spiritual vacuum. Today, with communism dead as serious belief system, China is coming to religious life once again.

Mao's communist guerrillas were militant atheists. As William Hinton, whose chronicles of the fictionalized "Long Bow Village" in Shanxi [Shansi] have become classics of a sort, put it, "The Eighth Route soldiers do not believe in God. They oppose Catholicism, they tear down temples, they smash Buddhas. They don't even wear shoes."[10] Shrines, temples, and churches in their path were destroyed; believers were manhandled or worse. Yet on coming to power, the Communists could not simply crush religion. In the late 1940s, Mao spoke of tolerance and democracy. One of his appeals to China's educated classes was that he would be more democratic and liberal than Chiang Kai-shek had been. Many liberal Protestants, particularly those associ-

---

[8] See Michel C. Masson, *Philosophy and Tradition: The Interpretation of China's Philosophic Past: Fung Yu-lan 1939-1949* (Taipei, Paris, HongKong Institut Ricci-Ricci Institute, 1985).

[9] Liang Heng and Judith Shapiro, *Son of the Revolution* (New York: Vintage Books, 1983), p. 6.

[10] William Hinton, *Fanshen: A Documentary of Revolution in a Chinese Village* (New York: Vintage Books, 1966) p. 120

ated with the YMCA and "social gospel" approaches, actively supported him. Hence the lip service paid to religious freedom.

Article 36 of the Constitution of the People's Republic of China states, "Citizens of the People's Republic of China enjoy freedom of religious belief. No state organ, public organization or individual may compel citizens to believe in, or not to believe in, any religion; nor may they discriminate against citizens who believe in, or do not believe in, any religion. The state protects normal religious activities. No one may make use of religion to engage in activities that disrupt public order, impair the health of citizens, or interfere with the educational system of the state….Religious bodies and religious affairs are not subject to foreign domination."[11]

That might seem straightforward enough, but the guarantees have in fact served as a rubric for a half-century of conflict that shows no sign of ending. Religion—other than the Marxist religion—simply has no place in a communist state. Beverley Hooper observes: "Although the Communists' treatment of private enterprise was directed partly towards the eventual incorporation of many existing establishments (both Chinese and foreign) into the state-run economy, their ultimate goal in the case of religion—whether Buddhism, Islam, or Christianity—was its elimination. While officially maintaining that religion would eventually die away of its own accord in response to changing social conditions, they were conscious that this would not come about so easily in practice. If religion was going to persist in China, it would at least need to be brought under tight state control. 'Freedom of religious belief' therefore came to mean freedom to believe in religion, but not necessarily to practice—much less preach—it, under government controlled and directed religious associations."[12]

Initially expectations were high that just as the recovery of Chinese society would come naturally as soon as "imperialism" (on which everything was blamed) had been crushed, so too religion would disappear by itself after "liberation." Communists tended to underestimate serious religious belief, viewing believers merely as people with distinctive rituals and customs, rather like ethnic groups with distinctive dress and dances. Just as they underestimated what it would take to change dress—I well recall the dramatic change that followed legalization of the *qipao* or Manchu-style slit-sided Chinese dress in the mid-1980s—so they found religion less amenable to control and manipulation than expected.

Hinton described in his first volume the apparent success of an anti-Catholic campaign in Long Bow Village. He tells how the priest, Father Sun, fled after he was attacked and "badly beaten up." Eventually the power of the

---

11 Kenneth Lieberthal, *Governing China* (New York: W. W. Norton, 1995), pp. 345-46.

12 Beverley Hooper, *China Stands Up: Ending the Western Presence 1948-1950* (Sydney: Allen and Unwin, 1986), p. 110.

leading Catholic family was broken: "With the destruction of the Wang family the Church ceased to exist as an organized institution in Long Bow. Although scores of believers remained, many of them bitter and angry over the struggle against the Church, no services were held, no sacraments were administered, no offerings were collected. The sanctuary itself was turned into a warehouse for government grain. The great tower, minus its bells, was used only as a platform for megaphone announcements of village meetings and news of the world. The rest of the extensive compound was borrowed by various government organizations as temporary headquarters. Among these were the Anti-Japanese Political and Military University and the Fifth District Office."[13]

This took place even before the Party had even taken full control of China. Once installed in Beijing, the Communists instituted measures directed toward state control of all religion. Religious policy as a whole was placed in the hands of the Religious Affairs Bureau. The Chinese Buddhist Association and the Chinese Islamic Association were set up in mid-1953. There were two distinct Christian associations: the Protestants' Three Self Movement, which was launched in July 1950 but not officially constituted until April 1951, and the National Patriotic Catholic Association, established only in July 1957. Harvard researcher Holmes Welch's statement that the Chinese Buddhist Association was "used primarily as an instrument for remolding Buddhism to suit the needs of the Government" also applied generally to the other religious associations."[14]

Yet while a centralized structure was created to direct and control religion, the higher levels lacked authority over the lower. The former were solely a tool of united front politics. Churches, mosques, and temples came under the direct control of local communist parties and security organizations. The assumption was that somehow the believers would cling to the official venues and structures, like iron filings to a magnet.

Those who refused to go along with state control, whether they were Buddhist or Christian or Muslim, were ruthlessly hounded. Many were killed; others ended up in the Chinese Gulag Archipelago. But while the 1950s was no period of tolerance or coexistence with religion, some religious practice was allowed. This ended with the Cultural Revolution, and from 1966 until 1979 the practice of religion was effectively prohibited at a horrible human cost. Thousands of shrines, temples, churches, and other holy places were destroyed across China, and with particular brutality in the non-Chinese areas of Tibet and Xinjiang.

The results, however, were not as expected. The believers scattered and reorganized deep underground. Some individuals abandoned their faith but those who continued believed more devoutly than ever. The net result, as

---

[13] Hinton, *Fanshen*, pp.145-46.
[14] Hooper, *China Stands Up*, pp. 110-111.

would become clear when restrictions were lifted in the 1980s, was that although organized religion had been destroyed, religion itself had been strengthened—and relocated beyond the reach of the state.

Our best glimpses of religious practice during the Cultural Revolution period come from prison memoirs. The late Jean Pasqualini, a French citizen whose father was Corsican and mother Chinese, describes the saintly Father Hsia in the prison camp where he spent many years:

> Hsia trusted me to the point that he knew I would never report him, so he often lowered his caution when he was around me. Once I overheard an amazing exchange when a very devout Christian came to see him for advice about stealing. Like all the rest, he had been keeping himself alive by grabbing extra food, but the morality of theft still bothered him.
> "Do the guards know you people are stealing food?" Hsia asked him.
> "Well, sure. They know that foraging goes on."
> "Well, then," the old man went on easily, "if the government knows you are stealing and lets you get away with it, then the government is pretty kind, isn't it?"
> "Yes," the prisoner agreed worriedly, but that was hardly the conclusion he had been looking for. Hsia had been holding it back as a surprise.
> "Do you think God will be no better than the Communists?" he asked. "Don't worry about that anymore."[15]

This wonderful vignette points up the unanticipated result of the government onslaught on religion. The chains of command that bound priests and faithful in obedience to bishops and similar structures were destroyed. Father Hsia operated on his own, underground, as did his nominal bishop. Faith had become an individual and personal matter. When practiced collectively, it was in small groups where the bonds of trust replaced any formal institutional structures. The result was that when, in the early 1980s, the Party sought once again to grasp the levers of control over organized religion created in the 1950s, it turned out that the levers were no longer connected to anything real.

Still, a naïve and optimistic atheism informed government policy during much of the Cultural Revolution period. Hinton recounts how "the so-called 'Catholic Uprising'" of 1966 took place near Taiyuan, and how easily it was dealt with.

---

15   Bao Ruo-wang (Jean Pasqualini) and Rudolph Chelminski, *Prisoner of Mao* (New York: Penguin, 1976), p. 236.

The Catholics had built an organization called the Legion of Mary. That year they spread the word that the Virgin Mary would perform a miracle on a mountain near Taiyuan. Members came from miles around, from other counties, and even from other regions... thousands came, tens of thousands...a beam of light shone forth.

But security men found a man with a flashlight, exposed the "miracle" and "most of the Catholics repudiated their imperialist religion."[16] All according to the textbooks of "scientific atheism" and—as it turned out—all completely wrong.

The end of the Cultural Revolution left most of the mosques in Xinjiang completely destroyed and those few that stood were padlocked; the lamaseries of Tibet had mostly been dismantled by the People's Liberation Army, and across China proper village temples had been leveled everywhere. Those that survived were no more than shells, derelict and turned to other uses. That religion had been destroyed completely in China was widely accepted as fact by outside observers during the 1960s and 1970s. Christianity was assumed to be dead. As Donald Treadgold stated categorically in 1973, "The evangelicals' few Chinese converts were swallowed up by history, leaving on the surface of the clashing and mingling tides of western innovation and Chinese tradition scarcely a visible trace."[17]

But appearances were deceiving. Shortly after Mao Zedong's death in 1976 the commander of Guangzhou military region, Xu Shiyou, came to pay his respects. "When he saw Mao's body" recalls Li Zhisui, the Chairman's personal physician, he "bowed to it three times in the traditional Chinese manner. Then he leaned forward to look at the skin on Mao's chest. Suddenly, he turned to me and asked, 'How many *ga ma* did the Chairman have before he died?' I had no idea what he was talking about. 'Everybody has twenty-four *ga ma*,' Xu insisted. 'How many did the Chairman have'....To this day I do not know what a *ga ma* is. Friends who know more about Buddhism than I say Buddhists believe that every living body has twenty-four *ga ma*, but I knew nothing about such things."[18]

Clearly much culture—folk religious culture in this case—had survived the Cultural Revolution. Just how much became clear in the years that followed. Within a month of the Chairman's demise his chosen heirs had been ousted in a bloodless military coup and there began a process of mourning and reflection and searching that has only gained intensity since. In a quarter-century, the economy has recovered and scaled new heights, and political reform has been pushed forward and then pulled back, but the spiritual vacuum created by the

[16]   William Hinton, *Shenfan* (New York: Random House, 1983), pp. 282-83.

[17]   Donald Treadgold, *The West in Russia and China* (Cambridge: Cambridge University Press, 1973), vol. I, p. 69, quoted in Lambert, *The Resurrection of the Chinese Church* , p. 9.

[18]   Li Zhisui, *The Private Life of Chairman Mao* (New York: Random House, 1994), p. 21.

first three decades of communist rule has scarcely begun to be filled.

William Hinton's stirring descriptions of the end of Catholicism in the villages he studied turn out to have been entirely misleading. After himself returning, Hinton reported:

> [It] has become increasingly clear that Wang Ting-mo [his Party informant] overestimated the results of his campaign to eradicate Catholicism in Horse Square. By the time the Communist Party held its Twelfth Congress in 1982, Party and government leaders had convinced most people that they would again allow freedom of worship. Catholics who had for years been meeting secretly for worship, or who had not dared meet at all, began to hang pictures of the Virgin Mary on their walls, quite often opposite a portrait of the still-revered Chairman Mao, and dared attend Sunday services in the open. Horse Square today is as solidly Catholic as it was at the time of liberation in 1945, while the Catholics of Long Bow can still claim about one-third of the population as believers."[19]

Nor were Catholics the only group to return to old ways. Like many totalitarian regimes, China's seems to have imagined that if it relaxed pressure, people would somehow embrace the government in a way that force and pressure had been powerless to elicit. That proved incorrect. The tide of questioning and revival and reconstruction, which was really a matter of getting things back the way they were before the Communists attempted forcible change, has not ceased since Mao died, and the party has proved unequal to controlling or even channeling it.

In 1949, the Communists had made bold promises about what they could do for China, how they would modernize it and strengthen it. And for more than 20 years the Chinese people had watched them do their stuff—with the unexpected result that they were more skeptical in the mid-1970s than they had been in the 1950s. Communism as an ideology and system had simply forfeited any legitimacy it might once have enjoyed, and individual Chinese were left spiritually at sea, searching for meaning.[20]

In 1980 *China's Youth* magazine asked its readers to say "what is the ultimate meaning of life" and in its May issue published, under the pseudonym "Pan Xiao" a long letter that quickly became a sensation. The author described her own and her generation's despair and search for something:

> I used to have beautiful illusions about life. In primary school I heard the stories *How the Steel Was Tempered and The Diary of Lei*

[19] Hinton, *Shenfan* , p. 283.

[20] X. L. Ding *The Decline of Communism in China: Legitimacy Crisis, 1977-1989* (Cambridge: Cambridge University Press, 1994).

Feng.... But often, I felt a lurking pain and it was this: the reality my eyes saw always sharply contradicted what my mind had been educated to accept. I felt lost because I began to realize that the world around me was not so beguiling as it had been portrayed in books. I asked myself, shall I believe in the books or in my eyes? Shall I believe my teachers or myself? I felt full of contradictions.... My past education had endowed me with strange abilities. I closed my eyes, to talk myself into believing things, to memorize Chairman Mao's words, to hide inside my own pure and elevated spiritual world. Later, however, it didn't work.

As her disillusion grew, the narrator, a young woman of 23, recounts how she has sought insight or solace everywhere, but without help—from friends, from love, from philosophy, from literature: "My heart is so confused, so contradictory.... I confess I have gone secretly to watch services in the Catholic church. I have thought of becoming a nun."[21]

As this rambling and passionate document makes clear, religion is only one choice for China's disenchanted populace. A popular saying sums up the alternatives for loyalty as among the three *zong*: *zongzu* (clan); *zongpai* (political faction) and *zongjiao* (religion).[22]

Writing in the mid 1980s, Beverley Hooper observed, "The level of religious belief among young Chinese is impossible to estimate but it has already aroused the alarm of officialdom." A Chinese youth newspaper complained in March 1982 that "a religious fervor has emerged in some places. Even cases of female Communist Youth League members having their heads shaved to become Buddhist nuns have occurred. Young people should be warned that religion is an illusory flower, stated the article: Who has ever seen the divine power and the realization of the kingdom of love?"[23]

But religion began to squeeze even party recruitment. New Communist Party memberships in Beijing dropped precipitously between 1984-86 and 1987-89; in the same period the number of those joining Three Self Patriotic Movement churches had risen 170 percent.[24]

A confidential circular in 1990 reported that "religious activities and party activities compete for participants, compete for time, and compete for space." It said this phenomenon "damages the party's image, corrupts the will of party members, and seriously disrupts the building of grassroots party organizations in the countryside.... [T]he result is extremely serious." The circular called for

---

[21] Pan Xiao, "Why Is Life's Road Getting Narrower and Narrower?" in Helen F. Siu and Zelda Stern, eds. *Mao's Harvest: Voices From China's New Generation* (New York: Oxford University Press, 1983), pp. 4-9.

[22] Willy Wo-lap Lam, *The Era of Jiang Zemin* (Singapore: Prentice Hall, 1999), p. 123.

[23] Beverley Hooper, *Youth in China* (Ringwood, Victoria: Penguin Books, 1985), p. 165.

[24] Lambert, *Resurrection of the Chinese Church*, p. 236.

a "thorough reorganization" of party cells that had already come under the control of "religious forces." The document did not refer to any specific religious beliefs. According to James Miles, "Clearly the influence of Buddhism among Tibetan cadres was a worry to the party, as was that of Islam in Muslim-dominated areas.... A middle-ranking party official in Beijing itself, whom I had known for several months, told me one evening that he had secretly converted to Catholicism."[25]

An internal paper showed the attractiveness of the illegal faith in remote, landlocked Guizhou Province. There was an upsurge of Christian zeal in the backwater district of Bizhe. In 1991, 151 cadres joined the church. The number rose to more than 2,000 by early 1995. According to the internal report, even party members who had joined the Chinese Communist Party in the 1950s had turned to the church. One destitute veteran said he was attracted to Christianity because church workers took good care of him whereas party functionaries were only concerned with making money.[26]

As Vice President Wang Zhen told an internal meeting in February 1991,"Fewer and fewer people want to be enrolled in the party…yet more and more people want to join religious groups." In Handan county, Hebei Province, 813 people became Catholics in 1990 while only 270 people joined the party. And from 1982 to 1990, the number of Christians in central Henan province swelled from 400,000 to more than 1,000,000. Many of these new converts made the unheard of decision to withdraw from the party.[27]

Significant as they are, these decisions to turn away from official belief systems and embrace religion are purely personal. They do not mean that religion *as an institution* is gaining strength in China. Organized religion of every sort was put under Party control in the 1950s, as we have seen above, and when the Cultural Revolution's ban on all religion was lifted, reconstruction meant reconstructing the religious system of the 1950s, which had institutionalized control of all religious activity through the Religious Affairs Bureau and the local party and police. And, to be sure, when the temples and churches were reopened, many people came.

Former US President Jimmy Carter could report, truthfully and enthusiastically, "Although congregations must still register with the Government, membership in Christian churches is booming. The pastor of the church we attended in Shandong province knew of only 200 believers in his rural county after the Cultural Revolution, and they had no churches or Bibles. There are now 13 congregations in 11 churches, 2,000 members have been baptized, and Bibles are distributed freely."[28]

Christianity, both Protestant and Catholic, has indeed been growing by

[25] James Miles, *The Legacy of Tiananmen: China in Disarray* (Ann Arbor: University of Michigan Press, 1997), p. 181.

[26] Lam, *Jiang Zemin*, p. 140.

[27] Willy Wo-lap Lam, *China After Deng Xiaoping* (Singapore: Wiley, 1995), p. 153.

leaps and bounds. Outsiders monitor Buddhism and Daoism less closely but they too are developing. As Beverley Hooper notes, "Young people are more likely to hark back to Chinese tradition: Buddhism, Taoism, and popular folk religion. Some go little further than lighting incense sticks and praying at the recently renovated temples. Others are more serious. The son of one prominent Chinese official has taken up the contemplative life of a Taoist, at least in his spare time, refusing to go overseas to further his technological studies." [29]

I have visited dozens of Buddhist and Daoist sanctuaries and spoken with many young monks and nuns—and this is not to mention the great crowds of believers. Three visits over 20 years to the ancient Five Banyan Temple in Guangzhou have witnessed the transformation of what was in the early 1980s a stark and bare shell, undecorated and deserted, back into what seems to be an ancient and timeless shrine—with elaborate and suitably antique-seeming decoration, clouds of incense, and the regular chanting of Buddhist liturgies. In Fujian province, numerous shrines ranging from tiny roadside altars to multi-courtyard town temples have been entirely rebuilt, often with financial support from overseas Chinese.

In many cases, the practical work of religion is what first impresses people. Christians are known for honesty and selflessness—the very virtues on which communism once prided itself. Many nurses, for example, are reputed to be secret Christians. The Catholic charity *Caritas* in Hong Kong was first officially approached by the Chinese government because of its work in caring for the mentally retarded and others whose lives, according to communist values, were not worth living (and who were regularly allowed to perish, for example in state-run "orphanages"). High cadres, it turned out, had such children, and through those children they were brought face to face with questions of human life and love.[30]

Clearly religion has transformed many lives. I witnessed the crowd pouring out of the Basilica of Our Lady Help of Christians, at Sheshan outside Shanghai, after mass one autumn Sunday morning in 1999. Musicians were packing up their instruments after what clearly had been a wonderful service. Clergy, sightseers, old people, toddlers—all crowded the wide steps down from the summit of the hill on which stands the church (built in the 1920s and looking like a smaller version of Sacre Coeur in Paris). But it was the dozens of young nuns who impressed me most. They walked with the crowd or stood to the side, many in family groups with siblings and extended family, smiling and laughing.

There was something surprising to me about the whole scene. Suddenly I realized what it was. These people were happy. They were quite simply the

---

[28]   Jimmy Carter, "It's Wrong to Demonize China," *New York Times*, August 10, 1997.
[29]   Hooper, *Youth*, p. 165
[30]   Author's personal information.

happiest and most natural-seeming people I had ever seen in China, in perhaps two dozen trips over 20 years to most corners of the country. Later I recounted the experience to a friend who was completing a four-year tour at the US embassy in Hanoi. The same, he said, was true in Vietnam, where life is as difficult as in China. The crowds after church were the same: joyous, natural, happy—in a way seen nowhere else.

None of this should be taken as a "return to normal," however. The revival of religion is causing more unease among Communists in China and elsewhere now than its persistence after the victory of revolution did half a century ago. Then it was relatively easy to create institutional structures to co-opt and control belief, first because many religious figures took communism seriously and imagined they could work with it and also because ordinary believers had not yet undergone the suffering to come. Today, believers have built firm barriers between the heart of their faith and practice and official efforts to manipulate. Religion has become genuinely personal and social, divorced from organization and immune to the old United Front tricks—this despite the reconstruction of organizations within which many believers operate. For the government, this is very bad news indeed, for it means that the structures of belief and understanding of meaning, effective manipulation of which has been a hallmark of totalitarianism, have survived in China—and freed themselves.

Religious revival does not promise a solution to any of China's enormous problems. But what has become clear is that communism—which many people imagined *was* the solution, for 50 years—has now been discredited and discarded. I mentioned at the outset the passionate condemnation of Confucianism so characteristic of the China in which communism took root. Well, visitors to Qufu, the family home of Confucius and site of the grand shrines of his cult, could in the mid-1980s purchase red vinyl covered books in pocket size that looked for all the world like the famous "little red book" of Chairman Mao. But these said "Analects" on the cover and contained inside the sayings of Confucius. To say that anything had actually been resolved by China's 50 years of storm and stress would be an exaggeration. But a great circular path has now been traveled, back to somewhere not unlike its starting point.

The revival of religion in China is not a matter of organizational reconstruction. It is the product of a deep and widespread search for meaning in the past and the present—what David Aikman has termed "China's Search For Its Soul."[31] As we turn to China's present and future, we should note first of all that no governmental program can possibly provide the answer to a country that is in search of its soul. In most countries that search has been left to individuals in any case; for society as a whole answers can come, if at all, only from prolonged and painfully honest public discussion, and nothing remotely like

---

[31] David Aikman "China's Search For Its Soul," *The American Spectator* 31.3 (March 2000), pp. 22-25.

that is officially on offer or in prospect in today's China. Instead, Beijing is returning to coercion and propaganda reminiscent of the 1950s as it seeks to cope. The problem is that changes in the way state and religion relate to one another have made this even more difficult than it was half a century ago.

Beijing's current crackdown, which extends to every area of freedom, will certainly encounter no opposition from the current director of the State Bureau of Religious Affairs, Ye Xiaowen, who is known in China as an old-fashioned "scientific atheist" in the Marxist tradition. The crackdown acquired urgency in 1999 when followers of the Falun Gong numbering perhaps 10,000 peacefully protested outside government headquarters in Beijing—a demonstration that particularly unnerved the leadership because their own security bureau had provided no advance warning. The group in question follows a traditional-style meditation and exercise regimen under the leadership of Li Hongzhi (now in exile), who claims a variety of mystical powers but poses no discernible threat to the regime. The leadership, however, had been looking for a way to show how tough it was in order to frighten China's increasingly uncontrollable society back into line—to "kill the chicken for the monkey to see"—and the Falun Gong looked like an ideal target. It would be crushed, so the plan went, by the end of August 1999.

On June 21, an editorial in the *People's Daily* editorials heralded the campaign's start, demanding that the party's rank and file "uphold science" and "smash superstition."

Eight days later, according to the *South China* Post, a front-page essay "severely criticized Communists who had neglected party creeds and turned to 'superstition'".[32] Wave after wave of demonstrations and arrests ensued, thousands were in custody by early 2000, and perhaps two dozen practitioners were killed by police; but there was little sign that the Falun Gong was even much weakened. A number of party members turned out to be involved in the group, including a retired Air Force general who was sentenced to 17 years in prison. Meanwhile, it transpired that the author of the campaign against *xiiejiao* ("evil cults"), Jiang Zemin, had in 1992 "consulted Zhong Gong master Zhang Chongping to cure his arthritis and back problems."[33]

Chinese people and their organizations are no longer naïve, as they were in the late 1940s and early 1950s, about communism's nature and means of operation. The appalling violence of the Mao period, moreover, has toughened them immeasurably. So not surprisingly, the crackdown on Falun Gong has proved anything but a demonstration of government might. As Professor William Liu of the East Asian Institute in Singapore sums it up: "In spite of the crackdown, the long-term problem of a spiritual vacuum that has been created by the decline of ideological communism after the reform may still pose

---

[32] *South China Morning Post*, June 29, 1999.

[33] *China Reform Monitor*, No. 273, February 7, 2000.

similar problems in the future."[34]

Propaganda and violence, as well as manipulative policies reminiscent of the 1950s, are also failing to deal with other religious problems. In Tibet, where repression has never been lifted much, the police regime has been tightening since the late 1990s. According to the Tibetan Centre for Human Rights and Democracy, "China held 1,083 Tibetan political prisoners at the end of 1998," many of whom are "systematically tortured."[35] On October 31, 1999, Chinese police opened fire on Tibetan demonstrators.[36] Nor have the Tibetan people proved willing, as Beijing seems naively to have hoped, to follow their nominal spiritual leaders without question if the lamas concerned have been selected as children by Beijing and brought up to serve Beijing's interests. The kidnapping of the 11th Panchen Lama, Choekyi Nyima, now nine years told, and the attempt to substitute a Chinese-selected Tibetan child, have created outrage. On January 5, 2000, the 14-year old Karmapa Lama fled to India, proclaiming his support for the Dalai Lama and stating that in order to practice compassion, the most important tenet of Tibetan Buddhism, "one has to be free." Much was at stake, as the *Financial Times* noted: "The boy identified by both Beijing and the Dalai Lama as a reincarnation of the 14th Karmapa Lama in 1992 has until now personified a unique success for Chinese religious policy in Tibet. The young lama has met Jiang Zemin, the Chinese president, and Li Peng, the former premier."[37] Much the same story could be told about Islam and the Muslims of Xinjiang—except that "armed struggle" has already erupted there.

In China proper, the government is attempting somehow to bring Protestant Christianity back on to the "Three Self Patriotic Movement" reservation, but with little success. Protestant Christians have become self-sufficient and have no need for a government framework or desire to join it. Relations with the Catholic Church have been particularly fraught recently. Beijing has long sought a bargain by which the Vatican would recognize its "Patriotic Catholic Association" as legitimate (which would completely undercut the eight million members of the loyal underground church) in return for some sort of role in the governance of the Chinese church; and such a bargain has often seemed tantalizingly close. Vatican Monsignor Claudio Celli has held more than 20 rounds of talks with CCP officials. But for reasons that are still murky, in 1999 Beijing moved decisively to scupper such a possibility. Jiang Zemin did not call at the Vatican when he visited Rome in spring of that year. Then, in accordance with a secret document issued in August, a campaign began to burn and blow up Catholic churches, with priests and bishops taken

---

[34]   *Straits Times*, Sept 5, 1999.

[35]   Reuters, January 11, 1999.

[36]   Associated Press, November 11, 1999

[37]   *Financial Times*, 8-9 January 2000, p. 3;

into custody. Finally, in January 2000, the Chinese government "Patriotic Catholic Association" created five new auxiliary bishops at a Beijing cathedral just hours before the Pope consecrated 12 new bishops from around the world at the Vatican—a move clearly intended to insult him.[38]

Examples such as these could be drawn from every religious tradition in China and multiplied indefinitely. What they show is that the same contradiction that bedevils economic and political reform affects religious policy as well. The problem is that genuine progress in China requires an end to communism—which is to say, an end to state management of, and capricious intervention in the economy, and the scrapping of the one party, top-down structure of authority in politics. But in spite of the leeway permitted in practice, China's leaders still flinch at any changes in principle, even though the point has been reached where they are inescapable.

An imperial system, but without the *dao* (the moral way)—that is one way of understanding the political structure that Jiang Zemin and his colleagues are attempting to build in China. Mao Zedong, who might be called the *Taizu* or "great ancestor" and founding emperor of the communist dynasty, currently lies embalmed in an odd shrine smack in the middle of Tiananmen Square. (Embalming dead emperors is of course not a Chinese tradition; it arrived with Soviet communism and has roots in the Russian cult of saints. And in China, as in Russia, calls are periodically heard to give the corpse at the center of the cult a decent burial.[39]) Political slogans extol the current leadership. One of 50 approved for the PRC's 50th anniversary in 1999 was, "Rally closely around the Party Central Committee with Comrade Jiang Zemin at the core and work hard with one heart, greet the new century with new achievements!"[40]

In dynastic times China's emperors carried out solemn seasonal ceremonies at the Temple of Heaven [*tian tan*] and Temple of Earth [*di tan*] in Beijing. At least one of their successors is still condemned and ridiculed for his attempt to restore stability to China by seeking to found his own dynasty: Yuan Shikai, who was president of the new Chinese Republic from 1912 to 1916. Will he now be joined, one wonders, by PRC President Jiang Zemin? About 2,000 workers have spent the past year constructing a massive tower topped by a rotating platform that can accommodate 1,000 people in the west of the capital. At dawn on New Year's Day 2000, Jiang personally illuminated the sacred eternal flame at the newly constructed shrine near Beijing called, resonantly enough, the "Altar of the Chinese Century" [*Zhonghua shiji tan*] near Beijing.[41]

---

[38]   *South China Morning Post*, August 15, 1998.

[39]   Agence France Presse December 26, 1999 reported a four point demand for closure of mausoleum by Gao Hongming.

[40]   *Hong Kong Standard*, September 15, 1999

[41]   The "China Century Monument," *South China Morning Post*, November 22, 1999 p. 8; also "Jiang Zemin an niu, dianran Zhonghua shiji tan shenghuo" in *Shijie erbao [World Journal]* January 1, 2000, p. A7.

One major component is missing from this farcical recreation of Imperial ritual, however, and that is the claim of divine sanction. Powerful as he might be, the Chinese emperor acknowledged himself as subject to Heaven [*tian*] and to The Way [*dao*]. Expressing that relationship was part of the ceremony. The recreated ceremony, however, places the communist leader at the apex of authority. He is, as Mao once put it, like a "monk with a leaky umbrella"— which is to say, in a Chinese pun, "without law and without Heaven."[42] There was a time when many believed, and not only in China, that the state could make up that lack. Chinese experience—and they gave it a good try—has not borne that out.

---

[42] "wu fa wu tian"—literally without hair and without sky—since monks shave their heads and the umbrella would block his view.

Issues to Keep an Eye on

Filling the Vacuum. What sort of faith will fill the spiritual vacuum left in China by the collapse of belief in communism? Can materialism do it? What about nationalism? Or will the Chinese turn out to be like all other humans in history—concerned with ultimate questions that governments have difficulty in answering? Remember that the Chinese government has no abstract commitment to religious tolerance such as that in the American Bill of Rights. Quite the opposite: Communist ideology is explicitly anti-religious. Therefore, one must always search for a political context when analyzing Beijing's dealings with religion. Nothing is disinterested.

Culture. How is religion reentering Chinese culture? Do we find religious themes in literature and the arts? What sorts of programs and courses exist in universities? What sorts of books and magazines?

Islam. How will the story unfold with respect to Islam? The long-oppressed Muslim Uighurs of Xinjiang are becoming increasingly assertive and are developing ties with coreligionists (and fellow Turks) across Asia as far as Istanbul. China is responding with its army and police. Executions are regularly reported. Fear of "Islamic Fundamentalism" is one of the ties that binds China to Israel. Yet at the same time Beijing is Islamic Pakistan's closest ally. Indeed, China may have provided Pakistan with the first "Islamic Bomb."

Tibet. How will the persecution of Tibetan Buddhism affect China's ties with Mongolia and India? Mongolia shares the Tibetan religion, while India has a long-standing interest in Tibet.

Catholics. What will become of the "Patriotic Catholic Association"? There is no such thing as a Catholic who does not look to the Pope; genuine believers even within the official Chinese "Catholic church" have loyalty to Rome. In return for establishing relations with China, however, Rome wants the same sort of control over doctrine and practice that it has with the Catholic Church elsewhere.

Falun Gong. The strength of Falun Gong and the official inability to crush it reminds us that Chinese governments have repeatedly had trouble with similar faiths, derived from Daoism and Buddhism. Will the all-out persecution of Falun Gong actually crush it? Or will it simply harden the resolve of those members who have not already quit—as appears to be happening.

Confucianism. What is the future of Confucianism? This is by no means the fossil some portray. It is a profound moral and social vision expressed in Chinese of a quality that utterly overshadows anything being written today. Confucian attitudes are still widespread. Will the Confucian system of thought be rediscovered?

References

Aikman, David. "China's Search For Its Soul," *The American Spectator* 31.3 (March 2000), pp. 22-25.

Chin, Pa. *Family*. Boston: Cheng & Tsui Company, 1992.

Ding, X. L. *The Decline of Communism in China: Legitimacy Crisis, 1977-1989*. Cambridge: Cambridge University Press, 1994.

Fu, Zhengyuan. *Autocratic Tradition and Chinese Politics*. Cambridge: Cambridge University Press, 1993.

Heng, Liang and Judith Shapiro, *Son of the Revolution*. New York: Vintage Books, 1983.

Hinton, William. *Fanshen: A Documentary of Revolution in a Chinese Village*. New York: Vintage Books, 1966.

_____. *Shenfan*. New York: Random House, 1983.

Hooper, Beverley. *China Stands Up: Ending the Western Presence 1948-1950*. Sydney: Allen and Unwin, 1986.

_____. *Youth in China*. Ringwood, Victoria: Penguin Books, 1985.

Hsun, Lu. "A Madman's Diary." *Selected Stories of Lu Hsun*. Trs. Yang Hsien-yi and Gladys Yang. Peking: Foreign Languages Press, 1978.

Lam, Willy Wo-lap. *China After Deng Xiaoping*. Singapore: Wiley, 1995.

_____. *The Era of Jiang Zemin*. Singapore: Prentice Hall, 1999.

Lambert, Tony. *The Resurrection of the Chinese Church*. Wheaton, Illinois: Harold Shaw, 1994.

Lieberthal, Kenneth. *Governing China*. New York: W. W. Norton, 1995.

Masson, Michael C. *Philosophy and Tradition: The Interpretation of China's Philosophic Past: Fung Yu-lan 1939-1949*. Taipei, Paris, Hong Kong: Ricci-Ricci Institute, 1985.

Miles, James. *The Legacy of Tiananmen: China in Disarray*. Ann Arbor: University of Michigan Press, 1997.

Mote, Frederick W. *Intellectual Foundations of China*. New York: Knopf, 1971

Ruo-want, Bao (Jean Pasqualini) and Rudolph Chelminski. *Prisoner of Mao*. New York: Penguin, 1976.

Xiao, Pan. "Why Is Life's Road Getting Narrower and Narrower?" *Mao's Harvest: Voices From China's New Generation*. Eds. Helen F. Siu and Zelda Stern. New York: Oxford University Press, 1983.

Waldron, Arthur. "Religious Revivals in Communist China," *Orbis* (Spring 1998), pp. 325-334.

Zhisui, Li.. *The Private Life of Chairman Mao*. New York: Random House, 1994.

The Opium Wars of the New Millennium: Religion in Eastern Europe and the Former Soviet Union

Eileen Barker

One of the most unexpected events, if not *the* most unexpected event, to have occurred in Europe during the course of the 20th century must be the collapse of the Berlin Wall in 1989 and the collapse of the Soviet empire in its wake. One of the most heralded, if not *the* most acclaimed victories was that of freedom—political, economic, social, cultural and religious freedom. No longer were the masses to be robotic zombies—oppressed fodder for the Soviet economic base (an ironic twist for Marx and Marxism)—compelled to follow the dictates of an atheist regime, under the thumbs of the KGB, the Stasi, and their brethren. All were to be free to believe, worship, and practice according to their own consciences; to organize religious institutions; to build churches, mosques and temples; to enter into open dialogue with those of other faiths; to distribute Bibles and other sacred texts. The opiate of the masses was no longer to be a prohibited substance, but a precious nutrient, to be enjoyed by all who so desired.

Or so it was thought. We were not far into the 1990s, however, before it was clear that the honeymoon was over. Religious freedom remained a sought-after ideal; but it was our freedom, not theirs, that became the issue—except that the issue could be as much how to curb their freedom as to promote ours. What went wrong? In order to comprehend something of the battles that are currently being fought in the religious fields of Central/Eastern Europe and the traditionally Christian areas of the Former Soviet Union (FSU) at the present time, I would like to suggest that we need to recognize the singular effects of the removal of state imposed atheism, and the significance of three basic concepts: globalization, religious diversity or plurality, and nationalism.

The "secularization debate" has been raging in the literature of Western sociology of religion for the past forty or so years. Much of the debate is somewhat sterile because different persons have meant different things by secularization. There is no need to enter the debate here, but it has clarified some important distinctions that should be noted when we try to understand the present situation in post-communist countries. One of these distinctions is between what might be called societal or structural secularization and individual or cultural secularization. Karel Dobbelaere (1981) draws a similar distinction between what he calls "objective conditions" such as technological development, material-economic conditions, and the involvement of individuals in public activities; and "subjective factors," which would include the processes that facilitate the acceptance of a scientific atheist philosophy, of which atheistic propaganda, atheistic education, and the development of materialistic philosophy are seen as important components.

The societal approach to secularization is familiar to most students of religion in Western Europe. It has been defined by Bryan Wilson (1966: 14) as "the process whereby religious thinking, practice and institutions lose social significance." This process is normally characterized as being intrinsically interwoven with other social processes such as industrialization, modernity, urbanization, rationalization, bureaucratization, and societalization—and to both structural and functional differentiation. Others, most notably North Americans, have focused more on the world of ideas and their transmission, and suggested that these have been *changing* (rather than diminishing), so that while people are less likely to be attracted to formal, institutionalized religion, they are nonetheless still asking questions of ultimate concern and finding answers in new (or ancient) ways which may or may not be tied to traditional religious practices such as church attendance.

It has been maintained that "subjective factors" made very little difference to the decline in religiosity in Soviet times—the contention being that "objective conditions" (including what Marxists might refer to as the economic base and/or the material conditions of production) were all-important, and that secularization was "an inexorable process taking place all over the world."[1] I would like to suggest that while there has been a diminution of the importance of religion in public life in the ways described by Bryan Wilson—who does not deny the continuance of "privatized" religion as "a leisure pursuit" (rather than a political or economic pursuit) in modern society[2]—it might be helpful in understanding post-communist societies to ask the question: To what extent and in what ways might religion *re-enter* the lives of individuals who have been

---

[1] Dobbelaere (1982: 139) depicts this as the basis from which Ethel and Stephen Dunn (1975: 142-3) begin their explanation of continuing religiosity taking place among women and the rural population because of their exclusion from the mainstream changes of Soviet society.

[2] "In this private sphere, religion often continues, and even acquires new forms of expression, many of them much less related to other aspects of culture than were the religions of the past. ... [R]eligion remains an alternative culture, observed as unthreatening to the modern system, in much the same way that entertainment is seen as unthreatening. It offers another world to explore as an escape from the rigors of technological order and the ennui that is the incidental by-product of an increasingly programmed world" (Wilson, 1985:20).

brought up in societies espousing an atheistic ideology?[3] A further, related, question that might be posed is whether the societies themselves might appear to be undergoing a process whereby "religious thinking, practice and institutions *gain* social significance." In other words, whether a process of *desecularization* can be observed—to stand Wilson's definition of secularization on its head. While acknowledging that metaphors are potentially dangerous tools, might it be helpful to think of the shifts in the fortunes of religion in post-communist societies as analogous to water finding its own level after it has been subjected to an "unnatural" pressure?[4]

When we look at the evidence, despite the difficulties facing the traditional (and, indeed, other) religions, there can be little doubt that, according to a number of criteria, there have been several reversals of the secularization processes. The data are not entirely consistent and the statistics are not always as reliable as we might wish, but it would be hard to deny that the early 1990s saw a significant increase in individual church attendance and membership, as well as in reported belief in the existence of God, life after death, and other indices of personal religiosity (Tomka 1995: 17; Babosov 1997: 151ff; Kolodny and Philipovitch 1997: 301ff). Indeed, Greeley (1994) has claimed that the data indicate that in Russia young people's religious behavior, attitudes, and practices became more like those of their grandparents than of their parents.

Furthermore, when we turn to the societal level and to changes in state concerns about religious matters, we can observe the reintroduction of religious education in schools, the (at least partial) restoration of church property, and the introduction of laws that cover registration and privileges for recognized religious bodies (Ellis 1996; Sutton 1996). At least some of the churches have been playing a role, even if only a minor role, in the running of their societies—something which would have been well nigh unthinkable during the communist period (Anderson, 1994). And while one might not wish to argue the case too strongly, it can be pointed out that the role of the churches, albeit confused and confusing, has been more than merely symbolic in areas of conflict such as the former Republic of Yugoslavia and Nagorno-Karabakh.

The one exception (that could well be said to prove the rule) has been Poland, where church membership and church attendance would seem, according to some commentators, to have undergone a slight fall. The reason for this, it is frequently assumed, is that the strength of involvement in and by the Polish church during the communist period was "unnaturally" high. In

---

[3] In order to avoid the complications of treating Marxism itself as a religion, we may adopt the definition that Dobbelaere (1981: 38) himself used: Religion is "a unified system of beliefs and practices relative to a supra-empirical, transcendent reality that unites all those who adhere to it into a single moral community."

[4] I do not really like using the word "unnatural" with respect to social processes. What is meant is that the pressure was imposed by a ruling elite which has not been granted legitimacy by a large proportion of the population.

fact, the higher rates can themselves be seen as a function of the atheist state. The church supplied both an alternative culture and an alternative structure to that of the state. Self-professing atheists would baptize their children and attend mass as a statement of rebellion, or at least as a lack of acquiescence to the state's policies; forbidden *Solidarity* banners adorned the churches; church halls were used for political meetings and pulpits for political speeches.[5] Although the drop in church membership and mass attendance is not great, it could, nonetheless, be significant at a time when both membership and attendance has increased in those countries where the religion was more successfully repressed—the argument being that after 1989 the alternative functions of the church were no longer needed, those whose involvement had been politically motivated dropped out, and the Church turned its attention to other matters.

This is not the place to go into the niceties of what is meant, assumed, and implied by the concept of globalization, but as a preliminary orientation let us agree that it is a process that, although by no means new, has reached unprecedented proportions in recent years. It refers to all manner of ways in which it is becoming less and less possible to consider any society as an island "entire unto itself." Whether we are talking about the United Nations, Greenwich Mean Time, metrication, international law, international finance, multinational companies, use of the English language by airlines, transistors invading the jungle and the desert with top of the pops, Karma Cola, and McDonaldization, Reuters or the World Wide Web, the fact is that very few individuals, let alone any nation state, can remain unaffected by what is going on in the rest of the world.

Globalization does not mean homogenization. On the contrary. Although there are undoubtedly homogenizing tendencies arising out of globalization, there are also features that lead to localization, and heterogeneity. But the point to be stressed for now is that neither academia nor the media can hope to understand what is going on anywhere without at least some awareness of what is going on everywhere else on the globe—and, perhaps, the surrounding stratosphere.

It was in the mid-1980s that I first became aware of the extent to which the concept of religious pluralism might be a problem for countries unfamiliar with even the dubious kinds of democracies that are to be found in the West. I was at the University of Warsaw giving a lecture on religion in Western Europe and North America. Question time came, and a member of the audi-

---

[5]   It should not be thought that Poland was the only country in which religion provided a basis for protest—it clearly was not (Nielson 1991; Swoboda 1996). But it is not clear that the church elsewhere provided a statistically significant basis for resisting personal and/or social secularization in the sense that it seems to have done in Poland. It might also be added that there were several Poles who were critical of the extent to which Cardinal Glemp was seen to side with the regime in Poland (Stokes 1993: 113).

ence stood up. "This idea of pluralism in the West is very interesting," he said, "But who's going to win?" I immediately assumed that the translation of the lecture had not been very successful; yet when I gave roughly the same talk in Krakow a few days later, I got exactly the same question: "Yes, but who's going to win?"

Today, after a decade that celebrated the razing of the Berlin Wall, the breakdown of the Soviet Empire, and the introduction of democracy to Central and Eastern Europe and the FSU, the prevailing question has remained: Which of the many competing religions or ideologies on offer is to win? Battle has commenced, and among the main protagonists claiming the *right* to win are the "mother" or national churches. But before examining the religious wars in further detail, let us move back a step or two.

For North Americans and the British,[6] pluralism is normally associated with the more or less peaceful coexistence of varieties of Protestants, Catholics, and Jews, with Hindus and Buddhists accommodated more liberally in the background (although Muslims and "cults" tend to be treated with somewhat less generosity of spirit). Because of these connotations, it is probably advisable for the American or British commentator to ensure that he or she distinguishes between, on the one hand, pluralism—meaning the more or less peaceful co-existence of different religions— and, on the other hand, religious diversity or plurality—meaning no more than the existence of different religions. It is, furthermore, advisable to recognize the different *kinds* of diversity that have existed and still exist in Central and Eastern Europe. Very generally speaking, we might differentiate between three determinants of overt expressions of individual religiosity (or lack of religiosity) originating in three different socio-political historical contexts: before, during and after communism—what I shall rather crudely typify as ascription (the historical period of religious bondage), proscription (the atheist period of suppression), and achievement (the post-communist period of religious choice).[7] Today, elements of all three can be found in Central and Eastern Europe.

There were, of course, enormous differences between the countries of Europe before the communist period. For example, what was to become the German Democratic Republic, Estonia, and Latvia were predominantly Protestant; Poland, Lithuania, Hungary, Croatia, and Slovenia were predominantly Catholic; while Romania, Bulgaria, Serbia, Russia, Belorussia, Ukraine, Georgia, and Armenia had strong traditions of Orthodoxy (or the Eastern rite).

---

[6] Unfortunately this applies only to citizens of Great Britain, rather than to those of the United Kingdom, which includes Northern Ireland.

[7] "Ascription *vs.* achievement" is one of the alternative pairs of "pattern variables" created by Talcott Parsons (1951: 46-51; 58-67) to describe universal dichotomies that represent basic decisions underlying interactions between individuals and/or groups. Parsons' other pattern variables include specific *vs.* diffuse relations; particularism *vs.* universalism; and affective *vs.* affectivity neutral.

So far as internal diversity was concerned, again there were differences between countries—such as Poland, where the Catholic Church enjoyed what was (and is) pretty well a monopoly in the religious market; the erstwhile Czechoslovakia, on the other hand, has been home to Hussites, Lutheran Brethren, Jews, and numerous other religious communities alongside its Catholic population for a hundred and more years. A not dissimilar mixture could be found in Latvia.[8] Muslims could be found as significant minorities in Bulgaria and Russia, and formed the largest minority in Bosnia-Herzegovina. The point I would like to make is that most people's religion was ascribed as a result of birth into a particular ethnic group or geo-political region. What religious diversity there was tended to be very much tied up with geographical, political, and ethnic divisions. Certainly individual conversions did occur, but in the main these were to be found among intellectuals or among the political elite who had a secular rather than a spiritual interest in changing their religious affiliation—Henry VIII being not a bad example. But so far as the mass of the population was concerned, for much of Europe's history the practice referred to by the phrase *cuius regio eius religio*[9] predominated—that is, the religion practiced by the ruler of a region determined the religion practiced by his or her subjects. If a peasant or a serf adopted a new religion, it was more than likely because the local lord or king had changed his religion—or a new lord had gained control over the region.

More recently, when the great powers, negotiating international treaties, have got out their maps to redraw national boundaries, those ethnic groups that have found themselves unwillingly encompassed by an alien nation have tended to cling to their traditional religion rather than adopting the religion of their new country—partly as a means of preserving their original identity. Thus we can find Hungarian Unitarians in the Transylvanian region of Orthodox Romania, German Lutherans in Catholic Poland, and Armenian members of the Apostolic Church in the Nagorno-Karabakh enclave of Islamic Azerbaijan.

In short, if we want to understand why someone is affiliated to religion x rather than to religion y, we need to look not at his or her psychological predispositions or even personal experiences, but at history. To unravel the origins of ethnic diversity, it may in some cases be necessary to have at least a minimal historical knowledge of the religious wars associated with the Reformation and Counter-Reformation and/or to trace a group's history back to the conquests of, say, the Ottoman, Prussian, or Austro-Hungarian Empires, and almost certainly to the First and Second World Wars. In some cases, festering sores and

---

[8] According to its 1935 census data, 55 percent of Latvians belonged to the Evangelical Lutheran Church, 25 percent to the Roman Catholic Church, 6 percent were Old Believers, and 5 percent were Jews. Baptists, Presbyterians, Anglicans, Methodists, and other Protestants made up a further one percent (Krumina-Konkova 1998 footnote 1).

[9] Literally, "whose the region, his the religion."

resentments have been suppressed and lain dormant for centuries, only to erupt when the heavy hand of, say, a Josip Tito has been replaced by the trigger-happy hands of a Radovan Karadzic or a Slobadan Milosevic—and we know all too well of the bloody battles that have been fought and are still being fought on the territory of the Former Republic of Yugoslavia.

While the atheist regimes of the Soviet period certainly worked hard to replace the opium of the masses with the opium of Marxism-Leninism, they were by no means successful in creating ideological homogeneity behind the Iron Curtain. Again, we have to recognize differences both within and among the different societies. While in all of Central and Eastern Europe institutionalized religion was certainly not encouraged and adherence to a religious faith could result in one losing one's job, being unable to attend university or even in imprisonment or death, the severity of the suppression varied according to both place and time. In Albania, churches and mosques were completely outlawed; in Poland, uniquely, the Catholic Church continued to attract believers (and even unbelievers) to mass each Sunday, and, as already mentioned, managed in a number of ways to provide an important alternative to the socialist state.

Foreign missionaries did manage to smuggle Bibles into underground enclaves of believers throughout the communist period, and a number of evangelical religions and new religions, mainly (but by no means only) from the West, managed to convert members of socialist Europe to their faith; but the converts frequently remained underground, or at least very low key. Some, such as Krishna devotees, found themselves enjoying the hospitality of Soviet jails—and a few died while they were doing so.

Then, with the collapse of communism, there arose the opportunity for an individual's religion to be achieved through his or her personal choice.[10] Instead of religion being imposed or denied from above, each person was invited to shop in the new religious supermarkets that were opening up throughout Central and Eastern Europe and the former Soviet Union (FSU). Continuing the economic metaphor, new producers and new consumers were, in theory at least, ready to produce and to consume.

The supply side of the potential transactions is relatively easy to understand. Competing religions in the West had reached what appeared to be a near-saturation point in the West. Here was a great new opportunity to fill up the gaping vacuum left by the overthrow of the atheistic states. Whole new populations were waiting to be saved, enlightened, brought to the Lord, to

---

[10] There are those who will argue that one's religion is never chosen—behaviorists and some sociological colleagues claim that it is pointless ever to use such concepts as choice as all our behavior is determined either by our genes or by our social environment; and there are theologians who would claim it is God (or the Holy Spirit and/or Satan) that enters the heart of the individual, who then finds him or herself in the situation of Luther at the Diet of Worms: *Ich kann nicht anders* (I can do no other).

learn the techniques of yoga, meditation, martial arts, or what have you. Not since the intrepid missionaries of the nineteenth century made their forays into darkest Africa had such opportunities been opened up to those who know The Truth.

While belief in the gaping vacuum was the motivating incentive for the producers to supply, the mass media were soon put to work to advertise the vast spectrum of previously unknown and/or inaccessible goodies. Once the Wall came down, not only Bibles, but whole rainforests of literature swamped the literature-starved peoples of Eastern Europe and the FSU.[11] The printed word flooded into the East in books, pamphlets, magazines, and other forms of literature, which were passed by hand to friends and colleagues, distributed and/or peddled in the streets, sold in markets, bazaars, and shops without the fear of censorship hanging over either distributor or reader. Through news bulletins, documentaries, plays, and other forms of entertainment, uncensored radio and television brought, and continue to bring, new ideas into people's homes and the workplace. Televangelists were beamed through the ether, and the Internet offered an international array of web sites proclaiming (and denying) myriad Truths.

Throughout the first half of the 1990s, there was a veritable onslaught of American Protestants and new religious movements from around the world (but usually via North America and Western Europe). Foreign missionaries came and set up their stalls, toting their religious, spiritual, and secular wares to the millions who had so long been denied the religious freedom—and diversity—celebrated in the West. Literally *as* the Wall was being pulled down, the Scientologists were there, handing out literature to the East Germans flooding through into West Berlin. Soon they were promoting courses on *How to Improve your Communication Abilities* and all manner of other skills necessary for the aspiring capitalist. Purification courses were offered to counteract the industrial pollution and the after-effects of Chernobyl. Unificationists organized trips to the West for students and those who were likely to occupy positions of leadership in the future; they held conferences on a number of subjects in comfortable hotels in the Crimea (now they are more likely to invite those who can themselves pay for the privilege to one of their mass "Blessings"); and, perhaps most seductively of all, they sent volunteers from the West to give free or greatly subsidized English lessons. Transcendental Meditators offer Transcendental Meditation; Sahaja Yoga offers instant enlightenment through the awakening of the *kundalini*; ISKCON devotees offer Krishna consciousness and Food for Life—often going to feed undernourished and starving peoples whom the rest of the world has abandoned in war zones such as Bosnia, Chechenya, and Nagorno-Karabakh—until they are chucked out for "threat-

---

[11]   The longest queues ("lines" for American readers) I ever saw in Prague during the communist era were on Thursdays when the books came out.

ening to undermine national solidarity." (In Poland, a concerned priest told me how he has to spend a lot of his valuable time persuading Catholics that it is better for them to starve than to break the First Commandment by consuming food that has been offered to pagan idols.)

The Jehovah's Witnesses and Seventh-day Adventists have helped the unemployed find work; and the Mormons have set up a thriving cement plant in the Republic of Armenia. The new churches that depend on American Prosperity theologians (such as Kenneth Hagin and Kenneth Copland) have grown apace. I attended a meeting of about 6,000 young and not-so-young enthusiasts in a large sports stadium not ten miles from Budapest a few years ago.[12] I went to another in an open-air venue just outside Yerevan about the same time. In both places, the congregation was dressed in Sunday best and, one after another, grateful converts with shining eyes witnessed to how they had succeeded in their careers and turned from poverty to (at least relative) riches once they had taken Jesus into their hearts. Just as in parts of the West and Latin America, the "Happy Clappies" are selling Jesus with the promise of Health and Wealth—and some people are certainly buying and prospering.

At the same time, on a much smaller but nonetheless significant scale, there has been a revival of indigenous groups suppressed under communism— the White Brotherhood followers of the teachings of Peter Deunov/Beinsa Duno in Bulgaria, for example, and Pagan groups in the Baltic States and around the Volga region of Russia. There has also been the emergence of indigenous new religions—the (quite different) White Brotherhood followers of Maria Devi Khrystos in Ukraine; the New Jerusalem in Romania; Vissarion's Church of the Last Testament in Russia; the Faith Church in Hungary; the Soldiers of Christ in Armenia.

Moreover, while it is fairly evident when information about a particular religion is more freely available, it might also be noted that the supply of new ideas is not always so obviously tied to a particular organization. Concepts such as salvation, Armageddon, reincarnation, vegetarianism, ecological awareness, "the god within," and an awareness of the existence of practices such as meditation or yoga have entered the general domain and are there, as resources, to be drawn upon once the religious or spiritual shopper enters the religious or spiritual supermarket—either with intent to buy or almost by accident because it happens to be there—thus not only meeting but also creating a demand.

The demand side is more complicated and can by no means be reduced merely to an insatiable hunger for spiritual succor, although after generations of starvation such hungers certainly existed and continue to do so. Rather, I would suggest, there are a number of processes that promote a tendency for there to be increasing variety in the kinds of religion that will flourish, or at

---

[12] This congregation of the Faith Church has now built an enormous complex where vast congregations gather not only on Sundays but throughout the week.

least exist, in any modern (or post-modern) democracy—as opposed to a theocracy, dictatorship, or other kind of totalitarian state. Not all of these tendencies are equally strong in all societies, but together they make it unlikely that diversity will diminish without considerable effort being made to control people's options.

The factors that promote diversity include some of those connected with globalization—with increased access to new ideas through immigration and emigration (not only of missionaries but also of ordinary people of different faiths), internal geographical mobility, and social mobility. The fact that fewer and fewer people have the same jobs or live in the same environment as their parents by itself suggests that the kinds of answers to questions of ultimate concern that made sense to our grandparents will not make sense to our grandchildren. The growth of the mass media, although it certainly has certain homogenizing effects, also offers the masses at least an awareness of the alternative options available—options that were known only to a relatively privileged elite in previous times. This is true of all modernizing countries, but especially of the erstwhile communist bloc, where so many restrictions were experienced. A further factor is the attraction (albeit ambivalent) of things Western—particularly youth culture and its emphasis on individualism and personal choice, rather than communism (or communitarianism) and Big Brother. As well as the economic changes that introduced the dollar ballot of the market (in place of the Gosplan of state socialism), or the political changes of a secret ballot (in place of the well-nigh inevitable outcome of soviet elections), there have been numerous cultural changes in tune with changing ideological preferences.

Although there undoubtedly were and still are those who believed in Marxist-Leninism as an all-encompassing worldview, it would appear that the vast majority of people who lived under a communist regime were, to all intents and purposes, ignorant of the tenets of its atheistic ideology. There were remarkably few who succumbed to the intense ideological socialization of the Soviet states. Few would admit—except in public—that they believed in Marxism. It has been said, possibly with some truth, that there were more Marxists in the West than in the Soviet Union.

In other words, there was not suddenly a gaping hole that opened up in the hearts of the people with Marxism being rejected overnight. Nonetheless, Marxism left its legacy in the minds of those brought up within its ideological framework. The population, like any population brought up in a fundamentalist or sectarian religion, had been taught to believe that The Truth existed. The Truth was not Marxism, but, nonetheless, The Truth was waiting to be discovered. And, again like those brought up in fundamentalist or sectarian faiths, they had had inculcated from an early age that there were sharp and crucially significant distinctions to be drawn between "them" and "us." The "them" might be the bourgeois capitalist imperialists or might be, and increasingly had become, the state apparatus. Either way, "they" was synonymous with "bad" and "we" with good.[13]

Of course, not everyone responded in the same way to the collapse of communism. There were those for whom the political, economic, and social changes did not lead to any fundamental religious change. Many had either rejected religion for Marxism in their youth, or had been brought up as atheists and saw no reason suddenly to accept a theological worldview; for all or most of their lives they had managed to live without God and saw no reason to introduce Him now. Others had never given up their religion; these were most likely to be the elderly and those who lived in rural districts. Yet others, while believing religion to be important, found themselves so consumed by economic problems that they decided, consciously or unconsciously, to put religion in the "pending tray." But there were also the opportunists who changed from being card-carrying communist party members to being church-attending Christians, merely because they believed that such manifest behaviors were a way of securing advancement in their careers and/or their social acceptability.

Then there were those who, responding to the end of communism, sought some institutional home for their religious and spiritual feelings. The majority turned to the traditional churches, but a small though significant minority have been attracted either to one of the new indigenous groups that emerged or to one or another of the foreign religions. Let us now look at some of the "thems" and "usses" who play the roles of the protagonists in the religious battles of the turn of the millennium.

With the collapse of communism, the traditional churches were confronted (again, in varying degrees) with a number of pressing problems—many though by no means all of which can be in some way or another related to the years of state-imposed secularism. It is not at all uncommon for the churches to be treated with suspicion because of their actual or perceived collaboration with the socialist regime. There was undoubtedly collaboration in several cases. But there were many, such as János Erdö, who were imprisoned for their faith; and several, like Father Jerzy Popieíuszko, were to become martyrs in the cause of religious freedom. It is also true that there were not a few clergy who played an active role in promoting the downfall of communism—one well-publicized example being László Tökés.

In addition, the churches found themselves with an inexperienced leadership. Taking holy orders was hardly a good career move during a period of state imposed secularism. What priesthood there was demonstrated a demographic imbalance, with a preponderance of elderly and poorly educated men supplemented after the removal of communism by the young and inexperienced. Furthermore, the atheist regime had prevented those priests who were able to

---

[13] None of which is to deny the exclusivism of many of the religions and individuals found in North America and the rest of the West.

practice at all from gaining much, if any, experience—let alone training—in teaching, evangelizing, politics, or pastoral care. Even when clergy may want to help, not only are few trained in social services or counselling skills, but the people are just not used to looking to the churches for this kind of assistance, the state having taken over responsibility for the education and welfare of its citizens. Furthermore, priests may be ridiculed by school children; and secular teachers, who may suddenly be told to provide religious education, are themselves uneducated in religious knowledge and usually reluctant to take on a new subject that holds little interest for them.

The churches as a whole had little experience of developing a practical theology—the Orthodox churches have traditionally concentrated on the liturgy as a carrier of ethnic identity, and the Catholic churches in Central Europe were largely conservative (pre-Vatican II) with little to offer in the way of answers to issues of current concern for their flock—although abortion has become a hot issue that many of the churches are debating.

Moreover, most of the clergy were, and are, poor. Most of their congregations were, and are, poor. Much of the churches' wealth had been confiscated; property had been taken away, with churches being turned into hospitals, orphanages, swimming pools, war museums, nursing homes, or places to store potatoes. Disputes over the restitution and the restoration of these and other capital assets may become particularly acrimonious when there are two or more claims for the same church or piece of land—or when the hospital or orphanage is forced to move to a worse location or to close down altogether. The church can become defined as uncaring, greedy, and more concerned with itself and its secular interests than those of the poor and needy, with material goals taking precedence over spiritual matters. In Poland before 1989, one frequently heard the phrase "the Church and us against them." Now it is quite likely to be "the Church and them against us."

Finally, generations had been subjected to an anti-religious socialization. This by no means inevitably resulted in anti-religious sentiments. In fact, I have found remarkably little in the way of successfully implanted antagonism towards the opiate of the people—far less than the virulent anti-clericalism one comes across in parts of France or Italy, for example. However, it did mean that there existed, and to a very considerable extent still exists, a widespread ignorance of religious teaching and practice. The anti-religious socialization did manage to produce generations of persons with little or no knowledge of their religious traditions and rituals, unversed in the basic tenets of the Bible, and unfamiliar with religious or spiritual concepts with which to explore the transcendent. After numerous inquiries among intellectuals in Armenia, one of the most staunchly Christian nations, the first person I found who could name as many as three of the Gospels was the head of the communist party; and the first person I could find naming all four Evangelists was a young student who had joined one of the new Protestant religions that had sent missionaries to

Yerevan the previous year.

Given these and a myriad other problems, it is not surprising that the traditional churches bitterly resent the incursion into their territory of foreign nationals—particularly the American evangelical Protestants and new religious movements—but also any other competition. It is, the traditional churches complain, grossly unfair competition from intruders who have not had to endure the oppression of an atheist regime; who have the advantage of a wealth of experience in teaching and proselytizing; and who can draw on an apparently bottomless reserve of financial funds and other resources with which they are able to lure and bribe their innocent victims. Why, the national churches indignantly ask, should *they*—the interlopers from foreign lands—bring their newfangled belief systems and strange ways to *us* (the Russian, Bulgarian, Armenian, etc. peoples) who have been devoutly celebrating Christianity in our homeland throughout the centuries—and long before many of these foreign invaders' lands were Christianized, or even civilized?

All is not fair in love and plurality. The foreign missionaries are, the argument goes, bribing our flock—the flock that rightly belongs to us. "If a father has been imprisoned, is it not right that once he is released he should be allowed to have his own children returned to him?" the Mother Church complains. "Why should foster parents be allowed to steal them from us? The Jehovah's Witnesses (or Mormons, Moonies, or Baptists) are very rich. They promise the poor, 'If you join us, we'll help you with money to start up a small business'—they are *buying* souls."

Pushed into a corner from all sides with, they believe, the odds stacked heavily against them, it is not surprising that the national churches should fight back. And they have.[14]

One of the most notable things that has happened is that many of the churches have turned to nationalist sentiments to appeal to their flock and assert their right to claim them as their own. Increasingly the rhetoric within and without the churches is that to be a good—a *real*—Russian, Bulgarian, Romanian, or Pole, one has to be a member (or at least a supporter) of the national church. We the nation and we the church are one. "They"—the others—are beyond the pale. "They" are not merely heretics—they are traitors.

My land-lady in Yerevan is a well-educated woman and one of the kindest people I know. She welcomes me as a long-lost daughter every year when I return to Armenia. One evening I returned home slightly later than usual and she asked where I had been.

"To the Hare Krishna Temple," I responded.

"Oh—they're not Armenians," she told me.

"Oh yes they are."

---

[14] I must stress that I am speaking in very general terms; there are plenty of individuals, including priests, within the national churches to whom what I am about to say does not apply.

"No they're not."

"Yes they are."

"They're *not*."

"Look," I said. "They have all lived in Yerevan all their lives, they speak no other language than Armenian, and their names all end in -ian."

"They're not Armenian. They're not Christian."

"Come off it," I countered. "Your children aren't Christian, they're atheists. Aren't *they* Armenian?"

"Yes of course they are," she replied indignantly. "They're *Christian* atheists."

And that, it seemed, meant that they, unlike the devotees, were Armenian.

I was not entirely surprised to learn some weeks later that the Krishna temple I had visited had been desecrated. Several of the devotees had been beaten up and their property stolen or destroyed. A few months later, the temple was once again desecrated. One of the devotees whom I re-interviewed showed me a couple of photos that someone had taken shortly after. He had blood pouring down his head; other devotees were still in hospital. Someone at the American Embassy confirmed his story for me.

And it was not only Krishnas who had been attacked. In the relative safety of Moscow I spoke to a couple of young members of the Family (the erstwhile Children of God) who had taken a threat to throw them from their 12th floor Yerevan balcony seriously. They left the country within the hour. Nor was it just the new religions. American Baptists were not excluded. Young paramilitaries had broken into the homes and offices of almost all the religions in the country, except the Armenian Apostolic Church (of course) and the Mormons. When I asked the Yerevan Mormons how they had managed to escape, they told me it was because God was on their side—but somehow I suspect that the cement factory they run might have had more to do with it.

I questioned scores of Armenians about the incidents. A few were angry and ashamed. Some denied that such a thing had happened or could happen. But the majority (including politicians and clergy) said that while it was a regrettable incident, members of these foreign religions were asking for trouble—and that it would be best for them and the country if they (including those treacherous Armenian citizens who were denying the true faith that was the birthright of all Armenians) were all to get out of the homeland as soon as possible.

It is important to stress that these people are not *religious* fanatics. Most of them never go to church and, as already intimated, are incapable of naming the four Gospels. They are not vicious or unkind people. They merely knew that Armenia was under threat from foreign religions.

This story has been told about Armenia—but variations could be told about Russians, Bulgarians, and various other nationals around the world. In Ukraine, the fact that there are three Orthodox churches complicates the issue, since the three tend to hate each other more than they hate other religious bodies. But the Ukrainian parliament has had before it a proposal to outlaw psychologically destructive religions—generally taken to mean cults—particularly, but by no means only, the Great White Brotherhood.

I have suggested that a rhetoric to be found in many countries defines "us" in terms of—or, rather, as coterminous with—the members or supporters of the national/mother churches. All others are "them." But that is when it is the supporters of the mother churches who are talking. The story becomes more complicated when we look at "them" a bit more closely. Now we can find a discernible pattern of rhetoric which exhibits a similar *form* but different *content* according to who is talking. To generalize rather grossly, let us look for a moment at the other historically national religions—the Muslims in Russia, the Greek Orthodox in Albania, the Unitarians in Romania, and occasionally (though their case is somewhat different) the Jews in Poland, Hungary, Russia, and the Czech Republic. They, although not part of the "us" of the mother churches, may be heard to define "us" not just as themselves but as themselves *and* the national churches. It is *other* religions that they refer to as "them."

Then, listening to foreign missionaries from mainstream churches (the Baptists in Romania, the Lutherans and Anglicans in Russia, the Catholics in Ukraine), we can hear them talk about how they are working with the national churches to save the society for God. They are including themselves in the "us" with the mainstream traditional churches of the country—it is the new-fangled "others" who are "them." But we can hear a similar claim from the religions that emerged as sects in the 19th century—the Jehovah's Witnesses, the Mormons, the Seventh-day Adventists. They too define themselves within the expanded, respectable "us" of the Christian society.

This, of course, leaves the new religious movements. While Russian Rajneeshees, Bulgarian Moonies, Hungarian Scientologists, or Polish devotees of Krishna might consider themselves Russian, Bulgarian, Hungarian, Polish, or whatever, in the eyes of many of their compatriots and even of foreigners, they have denied themselves the normal rights of citizenship. By swearing allegiance to a *multi*national, global religion, they have shown themselves to be *anti*-national traitors.

An interesting postscript is that the indigenous new religions are commonly treated just as badly if not worse. They have not even multinational co-religionists at the end of an e-mail to speak out in their defense. An even more curious twist to the story is the attitude of some pagan groups in Lithuania, Russia, and Armenia, which claim to worship the *really* national gods—the gods of the earth whom the "foreigners" destroyed when they brought Christianity to change the land forever (and for the worse) a millennium or more ago.

At this point, passing mention might be made of the spread of the so-called anti-cult movement—an efficiently organized network of groups around the world that provides negative information about minority religious movements (which can include Lutherans, Catholics, and various other religions long established and respected in the West). There is no space here to go into any details of the way such groups operate, but their effectiveness in helping the media and, indeed, the population at large, to define the "cult reality" in their terms is by no means insignificant. While some of the groups set up in opposition to alternative religions have been started by anxious parents who have seen their (adult) sons or daughters change inexplicably overnight, the more successful groups rely heavily on networking with anti-cultists in the West who supply them with material, much of which is out of date, inaccurate and/or irrelevant for the country concerned.

Curiously enough, the more virulent anti-cultists bear an uncanny resemblance to some of the new religionists whom they attack. They present a kind of mirror image, in which the cults' "godly" becomes the anti-cultists' "satanic" and the "us" of the cultist becomes the "them" of the anti-cultist. For the anti-cultist, as for some of the new religions, it is all or nothing; you are either unequivocally with us or you are against us. To introduce qualifications is to "muddy the waters." Needless to say, such a perspective provides some titillating material for journalists, who, as elsewhere, are not slow to take up a good story.

But it is not merely the media, the anti-cultists, other religions, or an ignorant general public that can select and distort our image of minority, foreign, and unpopular religions. Pressure from a number of different sources is undoubtedly being put upon government officials to "do something" about the cults and foreigners. And it can be quite a popular move for a politician to join his (or her) people in the battle to save the motherland from the invasion.

As stated at the beginning of this paper, religious freedoms in the FSU suffered a serious setback with the progression of the 1990s. Not all post-communist societies have introduced restrictive legislation, but several have. Russia's 1997 law is probably the best-known example in the West, and several other countries have new legislation under review.

One way that the state may control religious minorities and, to some extent, religious majorities also, is through registration. States differ in the extent to which they consider this is necessary and/or desirable. Sometimes the law makes it particularly difficult for minority religions to register and there may be significant disadvantages in not being registered. Registration may, for example, require a mandatory minimum of 10,000 members (unless, as in the case of the Czech Republic, the religion is a member of the World Council of Churches, in which case, only 100 members are necessary), thus effectively excluding many minority religions. Another criterion may be the length of time the religion has been in existence in the country—with a period of, say, one hundred years (or, as in the Russian case, 15 years, which of course means before the collapse of the USSR) effectively excluding new and/or foreign religions.

While there are ways in which registration will provide positive assistance to a religion by giving it money or subsidies, and permitting it to act as a corporate body in law, registration can also function as a means of control—dictating, for instance, how the children are educated. Furthermore, not being registered can mean that a religious body is unable to hire a hall for meetings, or even to use its own premises for acts of worship. This may mean that it cannot operate as a religious organization in that society at all.

But even if the legislature does not discriminate against the religions—and several post-communist constitutions are exemplary in their scrupulous care not to do so—the *implementation* of the law may be less than fair. There have been numerous instances recorded of this being the case. Nor do states need to pass discriminatory laws to contribute to the country's capacity to discriminate. They can, for example, set up a commission to write a report containing highly questionable information which can be used as a basis for discriminatory actions.[15]

So what lies ahead for religion in the FSU? The very fact that so very few predicted the fall of the Berlin Wall in 1989 should be warning enough that we would be foolish to predict what will happen next month, let alone next year. We can, however, try to prepare ourselves with certain questions so that we can recognize the answers when they present themselves.

Perhaps we should also recognize that feelings towards the West in general and the United States in particular seem, after the initial honeymoon, to be increasingly ambivalent and defensive. It is undoubtedly true that there are increasingly critical reports in the West of restrictions being imposed on religious minorities and of foreign missionaries being evicted and/or having their visas refused. The introduction of new legislation such as the 1997 Russian law on religion has received an especially critical reception in the West from various quarters such as Oxford's Keston Institute, with the newly formed U.S. Advisory Committee on Religious Freedom Abroad citing it as an example of how government actions can threaten faith groups and how, since its adoption, there have been increasing reports of efforts by local officials to restrict activities of religious minorities.

As early as 1994 one could find a journalist being told by an influential member of the Moscow Patriarchy that "the West, first and foremost the United States" had spent "billions of dollars" in an effort to "vitiate Russia's spiritual vigour." Foreign evangelical preachers in Russia were "CIA agents." The journalist was, moreover, told in no uncertain terms: "You are

---

[15]This is a procedure by no means confined to post-communist Europe, as anyone with knowledge of the Belgian and French reports on "sects" will be aware. Such reports can, however, have some uses; my graduate students now have an exercise in which they have had to write 1,500-word critiques of the depiction of minority religions in a 1996 Report written by the Russian Ministry of Health Care and Pharmacy. Each year they have enthusiastically torn to pieces this extraordinarily rich hotchpotch of gross distortions, generalizations, inconsistencies, and inaccuracies.

from the West. I am an Orthodox believer. Much of what I say you will never understand."[16]

There are many reasons for feelings of ambivalence, but one contributing factor is undoubtedly the impression that the American media's reporting of the religious situation in Europe has adopted a holier-than-thou attitude that is offensive and displays a lamentable lack of understanding of what is happening now and what has happened in the past. One of the consequences of this perceived misunderstanding could well be that, instead of helping the progress of democracy, pluralism, and the implementation of human rights as laid down in the United Nations Declaration and other international agreements, the Western media risk providing ammunition to prolong or even exacerbate the opium wars of the new millennium.

---

[16] London *Telegraph*, May 1, 1994.

Issues to Keep an Eye on

Legacies of Communism. The effects of state-imposed secularism are still with us, although perhaps less obviously so than they were in the early 1990s. Still we can ask about the legacy of socialism and how far, and in what ways, it continues to affect the post-socialist generation. To what extent are religious beliefs, practices, and organizations becoming more or less important at both the individual and the societal level? Is the general population becoming re-educated in the schools? Are young men training for the priesthood? Are priests taking on more pastoral or welfare roles for their flock? How are the traditional churches coping with their newly found freedom? How successful are they in retrieving the property that was taken from them? Is internal politi-cizing leading to schism, revivalism, and/or increasing monopolies of power? And what is the relationship between church and state?

Diversity. To what extent is there a continuing increase in the religious diver-sity of post-communist society, or have some of the religions that crossed the Berlin Wall now returned whence they came? Is it becoming increasingly dif-ficult for foreign missionaries to obtain visas? Is whatever diversity there is due to a more marked adherence to ethnic boundaries, or to individuals choosing new religious beliefs and practices from the variety of imported and/or new indigenous religions that have become available? How far can one recognize alternative spiritual concepts and techniques available as resources in a gener-al cultural milieu that individuals can "plug into" without necessarily becom-ing adherents of any particular organization? Do the religious organizations cooperate with each other, or is there bitter competition between them?

Legal Developments. Are new constitutions being established, or are new laws being passed that address religious issues? If changes in the law are being introduced, do they draw distinctions between different religions? If so, what are the criteria that are used: whether they are indigenous or foreign? how many members they can muster? how long they have been in the country? What is the position of those who declare themselves conscientious objectors on religious grounds? Is the law applied in similar fashion throughout the dif-ferent regions of the society? What other interest groups attack or defend reli-gious groups? What role do the media play? How impartial are the law enforcers and the courts? Is there an organized "anti-cult movement"?

The Uses of Religion. What are some of the ways in which religion is "used" to further the aims of particular interest groups? Does it provide a symbol for national identity? How far is this evidenced by the erection of national monu-ments such as the Church of Christ the Savior in Moscow?

The International Context. Apart from the presence of foreign missionaries, in what ways does the rest of the world impinge upon the religious life of post-communist societies? Does the presence of transnational religious bodies significantly affect the functioning of the society and, if so, in what ways? What are the reasons for the increasing ambivalence that is felt towards the West with respect to religion? When the US government puts pressure on a post-communist society because of its human rights record, does this exacerbate or ameliorate the situation? How does the desire to become a member of the European Union affect the way in which a society treats its minority religions?

References

Anderson, John. 1994. *Religion, State and Politics in the Soviet Union and Successor States*, Cambridge University Press.

Babosov, Eugeniy. 1997. "The Revivial of Religion in Belarus" pp. 151-161 in Irena Borowik and Grzegorz Babi?ski, eds., *New Religious Phenomena in Central and Eastern Europe.*

Dobbelaere, K. 1981. *Secularization: A Multi-Dimensional Concept*, London: Sage.

Ellis, Jane. 1996. *The Orthodox Church: Triumphalism and Defensiveness*, London: Macmillan.

Kolodny, Anatoly and Ludmila Philipovitch. 1997. "The Non-Traditional Religiosity in the Context of the Spiritual Revival of Ukraine," in Irena Borowik and Grzegorz Babi?ski, eds., *New Religious Phenomena in Central and Eastern Europe.* Pp. 301-131.

Krumina-Konkova, S. 1998. "New Religions in Latvia in 1997/8."

Greeley, A. 1994. 'A Religious Revivial in Russia?', *JSSR* 33(3): 253-272.

Parsons, T. 1951. *The Social System*, London: Routledge and Kegan Paul.

Sutton, Jonathan. 1996. *Traditions in New Freedom: Christianity and Higher Education in Russia and Ukraine Today*, Nottingham: Bramcote Press.

Tomka, Miklos. 1995. "The Changing Social Role of Religion in Eastern and Central Europe: Religion's Revival and its contradictions" *Social Compass*, 42/1 pp. 17-26.

Wilson, B. R. 1985. 'Secularization: The Inherited Model,' in P. E. Hammond, ed., *The Sacred in a Secular Age*, Berkeley: University of California Press.

Wilson, B. R. 1966. *Religion in Secular Society*, London: Watts.

IV

Islam, Politics, and Iran in Particular

Saïd Amir Arjomand

On the bright morning of October 31, 1999, I woke up to the news of the disappearance of an EgyptAir plane off the coast of Massachusetts. What the ensuing investigation showed was that the co-pilot had uttered the words, "I trust [put my trust in] God" (*tawakkaltu `ala Allah*), when taking control of the aircraft in mid-flight. According to a theory given wide currency in the first days after the crash, this "religious prayer" was a clear indication of the co-pilot's intention to commit suicide by plunging the airplane into the ocean with all its passengers. It is interesting to note that in the 19th century, the notion of reliance on God (*tawakkul*) would most likely have been taken in conjunction with that of kismet as proof of the "fatalism" of the Muslims. The old Orientalist image of fatalism and resignation, however, doesn't fit the new stereotype of "militant Islam." Instead, it is the fanaticism of the contemporary revolutionary Muslim which is depicted in the image of a terrorist with a crazy suicidal bent (and, if he is Shi`ite, an obsession with martyrdom).[1]

A few days before the EgyptAir crash, on October 20, 1999, `Abudrrahman Wahid was elected President of Indonesia. Wahid is the leader of the Islamic movement Nahdlatul Ulama, which numbers some 35 million members. A decade ago, the line of least resistance would have been to label his movement as "fundamentalist"; indeed, the one other Asian mass Islamic movement on a comparable scale, the Tablighi Jama`at in India and Pakistan, was so mislabeled in the Chicago Fundamentalist Project (Ahmad 1991). It is obviously good that the term has lost much currency and was not used to describe Wahid and his movement. But what is curious now is the near total omission of all reference to Islam in the coverage of his presidency. In prepar-

---

[1] A month or so after the crash, six Iranian scholars who had been invited to a conference by the Center for Muslim-Christian Understanding at Georgetown University—and granted visas under the State Department's people-to-people program—arrived at New York's Kennedy Airport. The immigration officers detained them for several hours and fingerprinted them "to insure that they are not members of a terrorist organization." The group said they wanted to pray; when one of them raised his hands to signal its beginning, an officer (according to the *New York Times*), said, "'Oh, that's what you do when you want to commit suicide,' an apparent reference to the theory that a pilot on the Egypt Air flight that crashed recently had prayed and then put the plane into a suicide plunge." (*New York Times*, December 4, 1999) The group considered the hours of harassment and humiliation at the airport more than enough and returned to Iran on the next flight. In May 2000, the Iranian soccer team canceled its engagement in the US in protest against the continued fingerprinting of Iranians entering the country that has caused a lot of ill will among the Iranian otherwise eager to visit this country.

ing this essay, I could only come across one incidental reference: "Mr. Wahid, who for decades headed Indonesia's largest Muslim organization and has been a brilliant eccentric."[2] Wahid has been an advocate of religious pluralism and democracy since he took over the leadership of the Nahdlatul Ulama in the 1980s. Can it be that the reference to Islam is omitted because portraying him as a "good Muslim" seems anomalous?

These days, the Muslim world continues to generate an enormous amount of news. On the day of this writing (March 1, 2000), the *New York Times* carried one story from Egypt on the reform of family law and the granting of equal rights to divorce to women (with the blessing of the Muftis of al-Azhar); and another from the northern states of Nigeria on bloody clashes between Muslims and Christians over the institution of *shari`a* (Islamic law) there. Meanwhile, discussion of the landslide victory of the reformists in the Iranian elections continued.

Islam is an important aspect of all these events, but in many different ways. Coverage of them would be distorted if we resort to familiar clichés about Islam, defective if Islam is left out altogether. The temptation to do the latter is as considerable as doing the former. Discussions of diversity in Islam that focus exclusively on ethnic, geographical, historical, linguistic, and cultural differences in the Muslim world—such as Edward Said's (1981: ch.1)—tend to suggest that Islam should be left out altogether. Said is obviously right that one Muslim cannot be taken as typical of all Muslims, and that Islam should not be viewed as unchanging. But diversity can also be understood without violating the integrity of Islam as a world religion in its various personal, communal, and institutional manifestations.

One may speak of far-reaching and radical changes in the Muslim world and yet relate them firmly to history and culture. The Ayatollah's theory of theocratic government (*velayat-e faqih*), for example, was an historical novel-

---

[2] *New York Times*, December 27, 1999.

  During the first three centuries of Islamic history, various Kharijite and Shi`ite sectarian movements played a very important role in the conversion of the non-Arab subjects of the empire to Islam. The prototype of Islamic fundamentalism, the Hanbalite movement, arose in reaction to sectarianism and the philosophical movement, and acted as an important force in the intensive penetration and consolidation of Islam among the urban population. From the 11th century onward, the mission to convert the population of the frontier and rural areas increasingly fell upon a new mass movement, Sufism (Islamic mysticism). Popular Sufism became the instrument of the spread of Islam both into the geographical periphery of the Muslim world and into the lower ranks of Muslim society, especially in rural areas. For centuries, popular Sufism offered a distinct variant of Islam that was in many ways the opposite of the scriptural fundamentalism of the Hanbalites. From the 15th century onward, popular Shi`ism adopted many of the practices of the Sufis, such as the veneration of the holy Imams and their descendants in place of the Sufi saints, and pilgrimages to shrines. Since the beginning of the early modern period, a number of Islamic movements have responded to the challenge of popular religiosity by advocating the revival or renewal (*tajdid*) of Islam by returning to the Book of God and the pristine Islam of the Prophet.

  Opponents of the Qutbists among the `ulama have compared them to the Kharijites. The revolutionary ascetics themselves, however, seem unaware of the striking similarity between their ideology and Kharijism, and resent the comparison. The mentor of Sadat's assassins, Faraj, was vehement in his condemnation of Kharijism (Jansen 1986: 179-180).

ty that in no way represented the essence of Shi`ism, as many journalists who followed the lead of a few academics said. Yet, the theory is totally unintelligible without reference to the historical development of the conceptions of authority in Shi`ism (Arjomand 1988). To be more precise, the juristic authority of the Shi`ite clerics had grown over the centuries, insuring their increasing independence from the state. In one broad sweep, Khomeini extended this juristic authority to include the right to rule in his theory of the Mandate of the Jurist (*veliyat-e faqih*). The theory could not have emerged out of Sunni Islam because there had been no similar growth of clerical authority and independence.

For many secular writers, reducing the religious motive to other factors comes more easily than respecting its integrity. V.S. Naipaul, one of the sharpest observers of the cultural politics of the non-Western world, could only understand the Islamic revolution in Iran as a parody of Marxist revolution. (Naipaul 1981) While Naipaul drew a perceptive picture of young Iranian leftists, his account did not capture anything of great significance in the motivation of the Islamic activists of the clerical elite. The same blind spot for religion mars his notes from a second journey to Iran nearly two decades later (Naipaul 1998: Part 2). Here I will try to suggest some orienting notions that respect the integrity of the Islamic tradition but at the same time convey the nuances and temporal variations in the relationship between Islam and politics.

It was with the 1979 Iranian revolution that Islam thrust itself upon the attention of the world's news media. An undetected revival of religion in the Islamic world, ongoing for some two decades, suddenly became conspicuous by its sharp political edge. Ever since that time, the impressive presence of Islamic movements on the political scene has been manifest in a variety of events, ranging from the assassination of President Sadat of Egypt in 1981 to the stunning victory of the Islamic Salvation Front in the Algerian elections in December, 1991 (and the subsequent ferocious civil strife), to the predominance of the Muslim Brotherhood in the Sudan in the late 1990s. This conspicuous advent of militant, political Islam must be seen in relation to other contemporary trends.

The scholarly literature on modernization of the 1960s and 1970s contained extensive discussions of three interrelated and overlapping processes of social change, but without any understanding of their impact on religion, whether in the Muslim world or elsewhere. It was assumed that secularization would result from urbanization, the spread of literacy and education, and the development of a public sphere along with rapid transportation, electronic communication, and the mass media. The evidence from the Middle East and many other parts of the world in fact shows these processes to have revitalized religion (Arjomand 1986). The effect of urbanization and migration into metropolitan areas on the one hand, and the spread of literacy and higher education on the other, was to increase various forms of religious activity, including the growth of movements for orthodox reform that can properly be called fundamentalist; the combined result was a dramatic entry of Islam into the public sphere. Many young people moved from small towns and rural areas into the cities to go to universities, and became Islamic activists in the newly expanding public sphere. The public space centering on the universities, the scene of activity of the new generation of students attracted to political Islam, became keenly politicized in the 1980s.

Like other world religions of salvation, Islam is in principle universalistic and has a tendency toward missionary expansion and intensive penetration of social life. Contemporary processes of social change, including globalization, simply reinforce trends toward expansion and intensive penetration of society that are typical of all universalistic religions. Nor are these trends swamped by fundamentalism. The socially propelled revitalization of Islam, however, has occurred in the context of the modernization and secularization of Middle Eastern states, and of national political integration and the increased involvement of the Muslim masses in political processes. The spread of international political culture and institutions, increased political awareness, and the exclusionary policies of Middle Eastern states in the 1970s and 1980s had a particularly important impact on Islamic fundamentalism and greatly sharpened its political edge.

We should remember that nationalism, socialism, communism, and fascism were integrative mass movements that arose in Europe, especially in Eastern Europe, in a period of accelerated urbanization, of expanded literacy and higher education, and of unprecedented national integration. Like the inter-war European nationalist and fascist movements, contemporary Islamic fundamentalism as an integrative movement has tended to recruit its members *both* from the newly mobilized groups and individuals from all strata of society *and* from social groups and strata dislocated or threatened by industrialization and the modernization of states—notably a disgruntled traditional bourgeoisie (Munson 1988).

The political dimension of contemporary Islamic fundamentalism, especially its pronounced ideological character, is the consequence of sudden national and political integration in the total or limited absence of representative political institutions. In this perspective, politicized Islamic fundamentalism can be seen as organized but uninstitutionalized mass political participation. The distinctive feature of this politicized variety of Islamic fundamentalism is its ideological character. The emphasis on an ideology centered on an Islamic state that employs *shari`a* accounts for the novelty of political Islam within the Islamic tradition of fundamentalism.

For at least 100 years, a variety of entrenched and aspiring political elites who were and thought of themselves as Muslims produced a variety of movements and ideologies that I have described as Islamic modernism. These include pan-Islam, Islamic nationalism, justifications of parliamentary democracy in Islamic terms, and Islamic socialism. But although it figures in all their names, Islam in fact played a subsidiary and sometimes only a decorative role. In the past quarter-century, however, the situation has changed thanks to national political mobilization that attempted to tap the spontaneous vitality of religion for political ends—as well as to emergent Islamic ideologies.

The political conditioning of the contemporary religious revival has come about through the agency of the lay and clerical intelligentsia. A body of publicists, journalists, and university students and graduates have created a radical Islamic ideology in contradistinction to the secular political ideologies of liberalism, nationalism, and socialism. Here, the search for authenticity takes the form of the search for the fundamentals of Islam, and all later and foreign accretions are seen as corrupting. The basic breakthroughs in the construction of a coherent Islamic political ideology occurred in the Indian subcontinent in the late 1930s and early 1940s in the works of a Muslim journalist, Abu'l-A'la' Mawdudi, who died in 1979. The Muslim Brotherhood in Egypt was groping in the same direction then and after World War II, but did not achieve anything like the same degree of ideological coherence until the 1960s (and under Mawdudi's influence). In the following decade, the main features of the Islamic ideology were adopted by Muhammad Baqir al-Sadr in Iraq with a heavy clericalist twist, and then by Khomeini's militant Mullahs in Iran—incidentally, not so much before as during and after the Islamic revolution.

While in prison before his execution in 1966, the Egyptian Sayyid Qutb remolded Mawdudi's system into a sectarian revolutionary ideology in sharp opposition to Gamel Abdul Nasser's monolithic secular state. This opposition accounts for the characterization of the secular state as the modern idol (*tighit*) and the vilification of its man-made laws as the instrument of imposing alien ways and destroying Islam. "The Muslim community," Qutb wrote, "is now buried under the debris of the man-made traditions of several generations and is crushed under the weight of those false laws and customs that are not even remotely related to the Islamic teachings"—this being the result of "the loss of purity of the first source of Islamic guidance that was mixed with various alien sources" (Qutb 1990: 7, 13). The primary function of the Islamic state is therefore the establishment of *shari`a* to the exclusion of all other kinds of law.

Qutb argued further that the profession of faith according to the canonical formula (bearing witness to the unity of God and the prophethood of Muhammad) together with belief in the Five Pillars (along with the profession of faith—daily prayer, the pilgrimage to Mecca, fasting, and almsgiving) do not constitute the only defining marks of the Muslim believer. The believer must, in addition, reject all *man-made* laws and governments, which are the foundation of the new paganism. Moreover, the true believers—the elect—must organize themselves into vanguard groups apart from the secular "Society of Ignorance" (*jihiliyya*) and repeat the original pattern of establishing Islam through withdrawal/migration, *jihad*, and conquest. Qutb's spirit of revolutionary asceticism spread among the sectarian fundamentalists who formed several *takfir* (excommunication) organizations in the 1970s and 1980s. These organizations generally excommunicated the Society of Ignorance and "emigrated" from it, as had the puritanical Kharijite sects (seceders) in the 7th century; they might therefore be called neo-Kharijite.

The Muslim Brothers were brought into the Egyptian political system under Presidents Anwar Sadat and Hosni Mubarak through much of the 1970s and 1980s, and in the 1990s were integrated by King Hussein into the government of Jordan; a few served for a while in the Jordanian cabinet (Robinson 1998) while rejecting Qutb's revolutionary sectarianism. With their exclusion from the political process in Egypt and Algeria in the 1990s, the Qutbist militant sectarians have been making news with attacks on tourists in Egypt and atrocities as bad as those committed by the other side in the Algerian civil strife.

Islam has had a fundamentalist tradition going back for over 1,000 years to the medieval Hanbalite movement that surfaced within the Wahhabi movement in Arabia in the 18th and again in the 20th century, and in the early 1900s in the movement for orthodox reform in the Middle East known as the Salafiyya. Political Islam has a family resemblance to this older fundamentalist tradition, but what distinguishes it today is its preoccupation with ideology and the creation of an Islamic state to implement *shari`a*.

The ideology of political Islam bears a striking similarity to the Orientalist view of Islam that has been subjected to severe criticism by Edward Said (1979). What was written by the Harvard Orientalist H.A.R. Gibb could easily have been written by the fundamentalist Mawdudi in Pakistan: "The community [*umma*] exists to bear witness to God amid the darkness of this world, and the function of its government is essentially to act as the executive of the Law [*shari`a*].[3] Said maintains that the "canonical, orthodox coverage of Islam that we find in the academy, in the government, and in the media is all interrelated and has been *more* pervasive and influential...than any other...interpretation." The result has been the triumph of one particular interpretation of Islam that is essentialist and misses "the emergence of new and irregular realities in the Islamic world."[4] In support of his argument for the pervasiveness of the Orientalist interpretation of Islam, Said cites a statement from the able *New York Times* correspondent, John Kifner: "In Islam, there is no separation between church and state. It is a total system not only of belief but of action, with fixed rules for everyday life and a messianic drive to combat and convert the infidel."[5]

This monolithic, totalitarian picture of Islam is equally congenial to

---

[3] Gibb 1970: 11.

[4] Said 1981: 161, 163.

[5] *New York Times*, September 14, 1980, cited in Said 1981: 11.

Qutb and Gibb, as well as to Bernard Lewis, who has carried the mantle of Orientalism in the United States since Gibb's death. Lewis's idea of the clash of civilizations, it is worth noting, was recycled a quarter-century after its original formulation to inspire Samuel Huntington's gory cartography of a clash that shows that "Islam's borders *are* bloody, and so are its innards."[6] No wonder that "the underlying problem for the West is not Islamic fundamentalism. It is Islam."[7] Huntington comes as the perfect proof of Said's argument that, given the connection between knowledge and power and the imperialist genesis and intent of its proponents, this conception of Islam "covers up more than it covers."[8] Nevertheless, one can legitimately ask if what this model of Islam covers is some significant aspect of historical reality.

The answer is that it does not. Gibb's assertion totally bypasses the thorny question of what "the execution of the *shari`a*" can mean—a question the Ayatollah Khomeini was forced to bracket after a decade of strenuous efforts to answer it (Arjomand 1993). *Shari`a* is not the kind of codified positive law that can be instituted but rather what Max Weber called "jurists' law," where different collections of rulings by private jurists are considered normative by different schools, and where law and ethics are *not* separated. All Khomeini and his successors have managed to do is to give "Islamic" sanction to an enormous body of state law that they cannot even claim to be fully consistent with *shari`a*. Khomeini's last revolutionary act was the creation of a Council for the Assessment of the Interest of the Islamic Order (*majma`-e tashkhis-e maslahat*) which can overrule *shari`a* in the public interest (*maslahat*). This opened the way for important divergences from consensual *shari`a* norms such as the introduction of alimony and the appointment of female judges.

The changes in the status of women in Iran, incidentally, are very interesting but often obscured by visceral American revulsion to the veil. Despite very keen interest in women's affairs and feminism on the part of the media, this revulsion—be it in traditional forms or in the form of the modified head scarf—often gets in the way of unbiased reporting. I suspect it at times even drives very capable journalists such as Judith Miller of the *New York Times* to consider the veil as confirmation of everything nasty about Islam and revert lock, stock, and barrel to the Orientalist image of Islam.[9] There are, of course, exceptions. The *New York Times Magazine* itself has published not only Judith Miller's alarmist feature article but also Elaine Sciolino's much more sympathetic "The Chanel under the Chador," with a two-page picture of the veiled

---

6   Huntington 1996: 258.
7   Huntington 1996: 217.
8   Said 1981: 163.
9   "The Islamic Wave," *New York Times Magazine*, May 31, 1992.

Fa`izeh Hashemi, daughter of the former President Hashemi Rafsanjani.[10]

In setting up the Interest Council to break the deadlock between the Majles (Iranian parliament) and the religious jurists of Iran's Council of Guardians, the supreme Shi`ite jurist (*faqih*) finally accepted the principle that public interest is the legitimate grounds for overruling *shari`a*—a principle the comes from Sunni jurisprudence. *Pace* Gibb, mainstream Sunni Islam established this principle of public interest over 1,000 years earlier because it understood that *shari`a* was not meant to be established by the state. As for Kifner's statement, while jihad is certainly present as a basic feature of Islam (though it has a range of canonical interpretation), Islam is surely no more messianic than Christianity; to say that church and state are one is a misleadingly crude way of characterizing the varying structure of authority in the long history of Islam on the basis of an analogy with Western Christianity. Yet the Gibb-Kifner view of Islam *does*, to a reasonable degree, correspond to the idea of Islam put forward by political Islam, and to a lesser extent by Islamic fundamentalism.

Trends in different parts of the Muslim world often move in opposite directions, since the conditions of different countries vary enormously, but we can cautiously say that the 1980s marked the climax of political Islam, and that since the collapse of communism and the ideological model of totalitarian development with it, we are witnessing a general turning of the Islamic movements away from the state and toward civil society. This has been no less obvious in Egypt than in Turkey, where new Islamic justifications of the market and democratic politics are taking the place of the theories of the Islamic state. But the most dramatic shift has taken place in Iran since the election of President Mohammad Khatami in 1997, and deserves to be treated in some detail.

It is truly remarkable that the regime set up by the Ayatollah Khomeini after the overthrow of monarchy has survived the charismatic leader of the Islamic revolution without any crisis of succession. This remarkably smooth transition was in part due to the fact that in the last year of his life, Khomeini resolved a constitutional crisis that stemmed from the determined effort to translate his theory of the Mandate of the Jurist into constitutional reality within the legal framework of a modern nation-state. Khomeini died in June of 1989, before the commission he had appointed to amend the constitution

---

[10] *New York Times Magazine*, May 4, 1997.

I am currently working on a constitutional history of the Islamic Middle East where several ideal types of political regimes in relation to legal institutions are being elaborated.

The Taliban and the above-mentioned declaration of the *shari`ah* as state law in some of the states of the Nigerian federation are the most obvious exceptions to this trend.

The trial of the police officers who attacked the student dormitories is just beginning in Tehran, and many expect new facts about provocation and preplanning by the forces of order and the disorderly Helpers of God to emerge from it.

This amounts to a very significant qualification of the categorical recognition of *shari`a* in the Cairo Declaration, inasmuch as most Middle Eastern countries are signatories to several such international instruments.

had completed its work. But the constitution was amended, according to his instructions, to include an Absolute Mandate of the Jurist (a new qualification); to recognize the above-mentioned Interest Council as an advisory body to the supreme jurist as Leader (*rahbar*) of the Islamic Republic; and to empower the council to determine the general policies of the state. Early in 1997, the Leader, Ayatollah Sayyed `Ali Khamane'i, reconstituted the Interest Council with a mandate to assume its function of offering advice on major policies of the regime, and appointed as its chairman outgoing President Hashemi-Rasfanjani. The clear intention was to demote the elected president by transferring one of his major functions—the determination of state policy—to the Interest Council. The election of Sayyed Mohammad Khatami to the presidency suddenly shifted this quiet trend to further institutionalization of clerical authority into the arena of contested politics.

After his candidacy was approved by the Council of Guardians at the eleventh hour, Khatami was elected the fifth President of the Islamic Republic of Iran with over two-thirds of the popular vote in an election with a very heavy turnout. His platform—the rule of law and civil society—was novel, and indicative of a new phase in the politics of post-revolution Iran. The rule of law (*hokimat-e qinin*) *was b*y far the most important and repeated slogan of Khatami's election campaign. I suggest we read this as an implicit contrast to '*hokimat-e eslimi*' (Islamic government), the slogan of the Islamic Revolution. Ever since the elections, Khatami's supporters and the pro-Khatami press have incessantly appealed to his landslide victory—"the over 20 million votes," the (nearly) "70 percent popular vote"—as the grounds of his legitimacy, and have referred to his election as a great, historically unprecedented event: "the epic of 2 Khordad (23 May)," the historic "national event of 2 Khordad," and the like. Although Khatami never disputed the principle of clerical supremacy as inscribed in the Iranian Constitution, the invidious contrast between the popular mandate of the President and the Mandate of the Jurist was barely beneath the surface at the beginning, and is now completely in the open. A novel and consistent political discourse has grown around Khatami's theory of political development under the rule of law, a discourse that stands in sharp contrast to the discourse and rhetoric of the Islamic revolution.

Khatami's election did not result in any new legislation (since he did not control the Majles elected a year earlier) and his Administration embarked on no major initiative (since he needed months to quietly replace the higher echelons of the state bureaucracy). The immediate result of his election, however, was the reopening of constitutional politics and the reexamination of the fundamental principles of order in the Islamic Republic. This reopening was signaled by the vigorous spread of a new, post-revolutionary political discourse, using Khatami's neologisms and others like them.

In November 1997 disgruntled senior Ayatollahs who had been pushed aside by the present leadership spoke out against the Leader, Ayatollah

Khamane'i. Khomeini's successor-designate, Ayatollah Montazeri (who had developed a theory of the Mandate of the Jurist that made the Jurist into an elective position in the 1980s) (Montazeri 1988), and Ayatollah Azari-Qomi openly challenged the Mandate of the Jurist (*Etteli`it*). Meanwhile, the former Speaker of the Majles, Hojjat al-Islam Mehdi Karrubi, whose wife and colleagues had been disqualified for candidacy in the elections, challenged the constitutionality of the Council of Guardians' assumed prerogative of determining the qualification of all candidates to elective offices. This broke the ice and enabled various groups opposed to the principle of clerical rule to voice their opposition with varying degrees of subtlety. During student demonstrations in the spring of 1998, this opposition was expressed quite bluntly. Two other influential former members of the clerical ruling elite who had retreated to Qom to teach and assumed the rank of Grand Ayatollah, `Abdolrahim Musavi Ardabili and Yusof Sane`i, were also consistently taking reformist positions.

The reopening of political contestation is most obvious in the vigor of current public debates. Khatami's government spokesman and Minister of Culture and Islamic Guidance, `Ataollah Mohajerani, removed many of the restrictions on the press, the media, and the arts; and a popular pro-Khatami press, notably Tehran Mayor Karbaschi's *Hamshahri* (Fellow-Citizen) and the newer *Jame`a* (Society)—which was closed down by the conservative clerics who control the courts—spread Khatami's new political language, to which are constantly being added such new terms as "pluralism" (*plurilizm, takkathur-gari'I, chandarzeshi*) as opposed to "monopolism" and "single-voiced (*tak-sedi'i*) societies," as well as "law-orientedness" (*qinin-gari'i*) and "law-abidingness" (*qininmandi*). This discourse has been criticized and mocked by the conservatives as a product of Western cultural invasion.

"I expect the honorable Judiciary," Khatami said in his inaugural speech, "to assist the Executive branch in the management of a safe, secure, and just society based on the rule of law" (Khatami 1997: 76). But there's the rub. The central paradox of Khatami's program of the rule of law is that the judiciary is, to use his words, in the hands of "regressive and dogmatic clerics." Until recently, the head of the judiciary was Ayatollah Mohammad Yazdi, Khatami's chief opponent. Yazdi, who retired in July 1999, showed no hesitation in using the courts to embarrass the President by imprisoning the municipal officials of some Tehran districts and finally the mayor of Tehran himself. More pertinent to our interest is the judiciary's intervention in the politics of contesting the principle of theocratic government, the very foundation of the Islamic Republic, by the reformist clerics themselves.

Political murders committed by the secret services of the Islamic Republic constitute a blatant breach of the rule of law. In January 1999, Khatami insisted on the arrest of a number of officials in the Ministry of Information (read Intelligence), including the powerful Deputy Minister, Said Emami (*alias*

Eslami), for a chain of murders of a number of writers and liberal politicians. Some of the conservative Ayatollahs were reliably said to have issued *fatwas* (injunctions) justifying the killings. The reformist Ayatollah Musavi Arbadili declared any such *fatwas* invalid. Hojjatol-Islam Mohsen Kadivar, a younger but prominent reformist cleric who had written a direct and detailed refutation of Khomeini's theory of theocratic government, delivered a speech in Isfahan in which he declared terrorism forbidden by the *shari`a*. Kadivar was arrested at the end of February 1999 and after a trial that became a *cause célèbre*, the Special Court for Clerics sentenced him to eighteen months in prison on April 19, 1999. The national press and student associations protested that the Court was unconstitutional, claiming that its existence contravened the international human rights instruments signed by the Government of Iran that disallow special courts for special classes of persons.

Toward the end of June 1999, Emami or Eslami was said to have committed suicide in prison while under investigation. On July 5, the reformist newspaper, *Salam*, published a secret letter from the same Emami or Eslami, containing the design of the restrictive press law that had just been approved in principle by the Majles, and which would put the press under the censorship of the Ayatollahs. The Special Court for Clerics immediately banned *Salam*, presumably giving itself the power to do so because the newspaper's editor was a cleric. Student riots in the University of Tehran broke out in protest against the closure of *Salam* on July 8 and continued into the next day. The Revolutionary Guards intervened, alongside the regular police and the hooligans of the Helpers of God (*Ansir Allih*), and effectively suppressed the uprising, but not before the protesters' slogan, "Khamene'i must Go!" was widely heard.

In reaction to the student riots, conservative clerics in the Majles pushed aside a bill prepared by Khatami's reformist Minister of the Interior to curb the power of the clerical jurists of the Council of Guardians to disqualify candidates for elected office, and in fact reinforced those powers. They also introduced a new press law providing for clerical censorship. Meanwhile, the notorious Special Court for Clerics continued its political activities unabashed, first sentencing the editor of *Salam* and closing the paper, and then doing the same to the leading reformist cleric, `Abdollah Nuri, and his paper, *Khordad*. The trial of `Abdollah Nuri in November 1999 provided the occasion for widespread questioning of the legality of the Special Court for Clerics as well as the legitimacy of theocratic rule and the Leadership. Last but not least, the clerical jurists of the Council of Guardians did not shy away from using their legally reinforced but vigorously contested power to disqualify some 600 pro-Khatami candidates in the February 2000 Majles elections.

It is important to bear in mind that the questioning of the clerical theory of government underway in Iran at the present time is just the political edge of a deep intellectual movement for the reform of Islam that was well advanced in the 1990s. Both lay and clerical intellectuals are conspicuous in this reform movement, which goes much deeper than the Islamic modernism of the mid-20th century.

If the rule of law as one of the two pillars of President Khatami's reforms has proved problematic, civil society (the other pillar) is, strictly speaking, unreal and does not reflect the actual situation in Iran. Nevertheless, the ideal of civil society cannot be dismissed; it stands for other forces in the constitutional politics of Iran under Khatami that are real and considerable. The Islamic revolution did relatively little to change the domination of Iranian society by the state that is the legacy of a half century of statist modernization under the Pahlavi dynasty. Civil society is an empty slogan if taken in the sense of an autonomous sphere of associations whose growth is facilitated by the legal system. The new press under President Khatami, however, has broken the taboos of the Islamic revolutionary ideology and is serving as the indispensable forum for a public debate that articulates a wide range of positions in the reopened constitutional politics of Iran. The advocacy of rights and democracy by the pro-Khatami press—which incidentally, like almost any other major enterprise in Iran, draws on state funds—has forced the conservative press and the proponents of theocratic government and revolutionary Islamic ideology to go beyond labeling their opponents in public debate as "enemies," "hypocrites," and "apostates," and to supply an explicit rationale for the positions most of them had not thought out. Nor is this emergence of an harassed but free press under Khatami the only major liberalizing trend.

In a major speech in April 1999, Khatami asserted he would use all his power to carry out his promises. He then proceeded to elaborate the third favorite theme of his new political discourse—political development. He pointed out that the pivotal element of political development is the recognition of the right of opposition within the framework of law. And he announced that the "first step in political development is participation, and the most evident channel for participation is the election of the councils." These councils were the unelected local and municipal councils provided for in the Constitution of 1979. As Khatami promised, the elections of their members took place, with the result that his supporters won a landslide victory with over four-fifths of the popular vote.

On the anniversary of his now epic presidential victory, May 23/Khordad 2, Khatami addressed a gathering of some 107,000 elected members of the village and town councils in Tehran and again emphasized the importance of political development and the need to struggle for "the consolidation of Islamic democracy and popular government (*mardom-siliri*)." He noted that sacred terms such as "revolution," "freedom," "Islam" and "leadership" (!) are "not the monopoly of any group." The Leader himself was pointedly absent. Pro-Khatami proponents of the rule of law and political participation included a coalition that has chosen *Mosharekat* (Participation) as its name, and was des-

tined to be the major winner in the landslide reformist victory in the national
elections of February 2000. It is now in a position to control the Majles.

Khatami's control of the Majles finally puts him in a position to counter
interventions by the clerical judiciary in politics and to give his program of the
rule of law some bite. It greatly strengthens his position vis-à-vis the Leader,
Ayatollah Khamane`i, and the conservative clerics, and should enable him to
initiate his reform program and be more assertive in foreign policy. Women's
issues are likely to figure conspicuously in this program, since women won six
of Tehran's fiercely contested thirty seats. Jamileh Kadivar, sister of the jailed
reformist cleric and wife of the Culture Minister and press sponsor,
Mohajerani, finished near the top of the list with the highest number of votes
after the President's brother.

So much for the overview of recent developments in Iran. What about
coverage of Iran in the Western media? Over the past decade there has been a
fascination with Iranian youth, their blue jeans and interest in Western music
and dating and holding hands in the promenade at the foot of the Alborz
mountains in northern Tehran. Christiane Amanpour's 2000 CNN documentary, "Journey to Iran," is representative of this continuing interest. I am very
gratified by this interest, since Iranian youth and its ways are very important
aspects of life in Iran. There are, however, other kinds of folks in Iran as well.
The pro-Khatami women in the Majles are not exactly Ms. Amanpour's party
girls, nor, I suspect, are their daughters. They will, however, continue to push
for the legal and administrative measures to improve the status of women, and
will keep a close eye on the courts administering the family law—the subject of
Divorce Iranian Style, an excellent if depressing documentary film by Ziba
Mirhosseini released in 1998. At the time of this writing, there is a sit-in by the
students of the exclusively female medical school in Qom to protest the poor
quality of teaching; this may or may not have the sympathy of the young
women studying in the Shi`ite seminaries in the same holy city.

What about the coverage of Islam in Iran? Sympathy for the reformists in
Iran is palpable, but it has the effect of dissociating reform from Islam. There
has been little serious reporting on the reformist movements of Muslim intel-
lectuals such as Sorush and Mojtahed-Shabestari. In the June 1999 issue of *Le
Monde Diplomatique* (No.543), Eric Rouleau published a very good piece on
this movement. ("Un Enjeu pour le Monde Musulman: En Iran, Islam Contre
Islam.") Peter Steinfels could easily do something along those lines in his *New
York Times* religion column, but thus far has not. The trial of Nuri in
November 1999 was covered quite well. The trial of Kadivar seven months
earlier, on the other hand, was largely ignored.

The student riots in July 1999 are perhaps the closest to a litmus test for
detecting subtle biases in the coverage of Iran. The story was never told as I
have tentatively reconstructed it above. Of course, I had a lot more time to do
so than the correspondents in the field. Nevertheless, there may well have been

deeper reasons for largely leaving out two important issues. The first is Khatami's clampdown on terrorism, which goes against the grain of the cliché that all Islam as militant Islam. On February 21, 2000, Kenneth Timmerman, a Washington lobbyist and self-proclaimed expert on Iran, appeared on the PBS's News Hour with Jim Lehrer to repeat the trite accusation of Iranian state terrorism he had delivered on the same program over two years earlier. If Islam is wholly terrorist, the clampdown on terrorism by a Muslim cleric— Khatami—is incongruous and cannot be easily integrated into the good story of student riots. For the same reason, the struggle over the interpretation of the political entailments of Islam among the Shi`ite clerics cannot be made to carry a significant explanatory burden. The student riots, and the reformist politics of Iran more generally, are good stories. Good stories have their own scripts. These scripts are typical narrative models for good news. But international Islam can only be readily accommodated in scripts for bad news. The line of least resistance is therefore to minimize the Islamic dimension or leave it out altogether. But this must be resisted. The challenge of current developments in Iran is to develop a script for the news on Islam that includes both the good and the bad.

Reporting on a single country often has more limited appeal than covering news with a global or international character. Islam as a transnational religion generates much news of global import as well as global anxieties of the highest intensity. Like the advent of political Islam, the unprecedented global integration of Muslims through the mass media first became apparent with the onset of the Islamic revolutionary movement against the Shah in 1978. The media contributed to Khomeini's success by enabling the Iranian opposition abroad to orchestrate widespread mass mobilization inside Iran. Khomeini's aides abroad and his followers inside Iran were able to coordinate their nationwide protests by using telephone lines, and Khomeini's revolutionary speeches were disseminated by way of audio cassettes throughout the network of mosques and religious associations. The BBC's Persian program sympathetically reported Khomeini's activities and proclamations, and these reports were avidly received by millions of households in Iran, to the dismay of the Shah and his political elite.

The international repercussions of the Salman Rushdie case illustrates the impact of the media on a globally integrated Muslim world even better. The protests and burning of Rushdie's novel *The Satanic Verses* by indignant Muslims began in Bradford, England. The Bradford protests were broadcast throughout the world and stimulated violent protests in Pakistan, which were in turn internationally broadcast and gave Khomeini the opportunity to reassert his claim to revolutionary leadership of the Muslims of the world in the last year of his life. Only a few months after accepting a cease-fire in the war with Iraq, which had been like "drinking a cup of poison," he had the final satisfaction of issuing the *fatwa* sanctioning the death of Rushdie, a non-Iranian writer living in England, for apostasy.

The impact of globalization on Islam is interpreted very differently by different observers. Eickelman (1998) sees the making of an Islamic Reformation in the spread of education and the growth of vigorous discussion of Islam in books and in public debates in the press and electronic media. According to him, the Islamicization of social life has been far-reaching but also dispersed, lacking any focus or single thrust. For Benjamin Barber, by contrast, globalization puts Islam in the front line of "Jihad versus McWorld." He sees the effect of globalization concentrated in a sharply focused and vehement "anti-Western anti-universalist struggle" (Barber 1995: 207). In his last work, the late Ernest Gellner did not make a distinction between Islamic fundamentalism and the general scriptural Islam of the cities, and considered what he had earlier called Islamic "permanent reformation" the major obstacle to modernity. Islam was in this later version a Protestantism of sorts, but its legal system atomized and stultified society and prevented the growth of political institutions (Gellner 1994). Along similar lines, Barber obliterates the distinction between Islamic fundamentalism and Islam. That the liberal Barber should thus join the cold warrior Huntington attests to Said's contention that the influence of the Orientalist interpretation of Islam had been pervasive. Barber's central chapter is entitled "Essential Jihad: Islam *and* Fundamentalism" (emphasis added). The emphasized connective is significant: All Islam is Jihad; fundamentalism refers to Jihad elsewhere, especially to the American Jihad against the global McWorld. It is Islam that "nurtures conditions favorable to parochialism, anti-modernism, exclusiveness and hostility to 'others'—the characteristics that constitute what I have called Jihad" (Barber 1995: 205).

The perspective of a global encounter of civilizations has much to recommend it. Contemporary Muslims see themselves as belonging to a civilization that grew up around Islam as a world religion of salvation that faces the challenge of the Western civilization. Nevertheless, I believe Barber's view of Islam is as fundamentally mistaken as Huntington's. Not only is there variety in Islamic fundamentalism (Arjomand 1995), but Islamic fundamentalism is by no means identical to all the contemporary manifestations of Islam as a universalist religion. One would therefore have to agree with Eickelman on the dispersion of the current trends in Islamization, whether or not one concurs with his value judgement that they add up to a Reformation. One important question remains to be answered, however: How does globalization affect the old universalism of Islam as a world religion?

Global integration induces many Muslims to emphasize their unique identity within the frame of reference of their own culture, which can be said to be at once universal and local or sub-global (Hunwick 1996:231). There can be no doubt that global integration has made many Muslims seek to appropriate universalist institutions by what might be called Islamic cloning. We thus hear more and more about "Islamic science," "Islamic Human Rights," the "Islamic international system" and a variety of organizations modeled after the United Nations and its offshoots—most notably the Organization of the Islamic Conference, which was founded in 1969 and whose last meeting in Tehran in December 1997 was attended by the representatives of the fifty-five member countries, including many Muslim heads of state. This phenomenon is a direct result of globalization. To confuse it with fundamentalism is a grave mistake. It is, however, a reactive tendency and could be called defensive counter-universalism. The relation of this to the old universalism of Islam as a world religion is analogous to the relationship between the defensive counter-universalism of Huntington's "the West versus the rest" (1996) and the old universalism of the Enlightenment.

The dynamics of Islam as a universalist religion have always included fundamentalist trends, alongside many others. The fundamentalist tendency in Islam has been reinforced by some contemporary processes of social change, including globalization, and it has acquired a new and sharply political edge under the impact of political modernization. Political Islam can also be considered a species of fundamentalism (Arjomand 1995). It would be seriously misleading, however, to equate Islam with Islamic fundamentalism. For one thing, traditional missionary Islam also flourishes, and has adopted modern technology to its growth. This is especially evident in the proselytizing movements in Asia and Africa. More importantly, the main impact of globalization on the Islamic world has not been the growth of fundamentalism but what I am calling defensive counter-universalism. Fundamentalism has been characterized as selectively modern and electively traditional (Marty & Appleby 1995). It therefore assimilates to modernity despite its intent. But the assimilative character of defensive counter-universalism is more pronounced. It has already resulted in the adoption of universal organizational forms, and (albeit restrictively) of universal ideas such as human rights and women's rights. It is difficult to escape the conclusion that, despite its intent, defensive counter-universalism is inevitably a step toward the modernization of the Islamic tradition. The road ahead is very bumpy, however. Let us briefly examine it in connection with human rights.

Whereas in the first half of the 20th century international legal culture witnessed some amplification of "civil" and "political" rights alongside "social" rights, the past half century has been marked by a "human rights revolution." This revolution has a strong international—indeed transcendental—dimension. On the one hand, most Middle Eastern countries have acceded to international human rights instruments, and all have paid at least lip service to the concept. The Preamble to the new Constitution of Morocco (1992), for instance, reaffirms the Kingdom's "attachment to human rights as they are universally recognized." Even Saudi Arabia's Basic Law of 1992 makes a bow in this direction: Article 26 declares the protection of human rights (*huquq al-insan*) in accordance with the *shari`a* a function of the state.

The number of non-governmental human rights organizations has increased in recent years. Among the human rights, the ones with the strongest social backing in the contemporary Middle East are women's rights. Women's rights are represented by official organs of the states, and by a growing number of national non-governmental organizations (NGOs) that are increasingly linked with international NGOs and the United Nations agencies. According to one report, women's NGOs stole the show from the state delegates at the International Conference on Population and Development in Cairo (1994), and delegates from the Muslim countries were conspicuous in the Fourth World Conference on the Status of Women in Beijing (1995).

Human rights include the right to religious freedom—which requires the decriminalization of apostasy. This requirement has been widely rejected by Muslim countries. Quite apart from the Rushdie case, there is an appalling record of prosecution and executions for apostasy and of the violation of the rights of religious minorities, notably the Baha`is in Iran and the Ahmadis in Pakistan (Arjomand 1996). But freedom of religion is also being defended by more and more Muslim intellectuals. Similarly, a growing number of vocal intellectuals have upheld Rushdie's right to the freedom of expression (Mayer 1994: 364-379). Others have insisted that religious liberty and freedom of conscience are clearly deducible from the text of the *Qur'an*. Nor is theirs by any means a weak position. It is the case that a large number of Qur'anic Verses state that "there is no compulsion in religion" (Qur'an 2.256), establish freedom of conscience and religion, and strongly imply a form of "natural religion" among human beings that entails religious liberty (Mottahedeh 1993). In Iran, `Abdol-Karim Sorush, the erstwhile chairman of the Council for Islamic Cultural Revolution, has gone so far as to put world religions on an equal footing in a recent title, *The Straight Paths* (*saratha-ye mostaqim*)—a sacrilegious pluralization of a fundamental Koranic concept.

On the other hand, the transnational Islamic resurgence has caused the assertion of the universality of human rights to be rejected, generating in its place an official "Islamic alternative." This alternative is embodied in the 1990 Cairo Declaration on Human Rights in Islam. As is to be expected in an imitative document, much of the legal terminology of the international human rights conventions is swallowed while quite a number of rights are in substance nullified. The Cairo Declaration offers no guarantee of religious freedom. It prohibits any form of compulsion or exploitation of poverty and ignorance to convert anyone to atheism or a religion other than Islam (Article 10). Article 22 of the Declaration bars "the exploitation or misuse of information 'in such a way as may violate sanctities and the dignity of Prophets, undermine moral and ethical values or disintegrate, corrupt, or harm society or weaken its faith'" (Mayer 1994: 336).

It is interesting to note that, in flat contradiction to the historical experi-ence and the public law of virtually all signatory countries, Article 19 of the Cairo Declaration provides, "There shall be no crime or punishment except as provided for in the Shari'ah." Article 25 further declares *shari`a* the only source for explanation and clarification of the articles of the Declaration. While endorsing the Cairo Declaration, the Islamic Conference of Foreign Ministers in April 1993 also confirmed "the existence of different constitutional and legal systems among [the] Member States and various international or regional human rights instruments to which they are parties." (Mayer 1994: 350) This acknowledgment leaves open the kind of insinuation of the international law on human rights into national laws that the Supreme Constitutional Court of Egypt has undertaken.

For membership in the international community makes the legal systems of the contemporary Middle East permeable to principles of international law, and introduces an element of legal pluralism. A process of osmosis is set in motion, not through the implementation of international law—we all know how woefully inadequate the mechanisms for such implementation are—but rather through the eventual absorption of the international legal phraseology of human rights into the constitutional laws of Middle Eastern countries. Owing to this osmosis, the seeds for future change in human rights in general and women's rights in particular have been firmly planted in the actual and potential contradictions between national and international laws, and especial-ly in rights-oriented international legal culture.

Issues to Keep an Eye on

The Iranian Debate on Islam and Democracy. Khatami's new political discourse has displaced revolution and Islam and put the rule of law, civil society, and participation at the center. Many of the former advocates of revolutionary Islam have radically changed their position and now see it as compatible with democracy, pluralism, and individual liberty. Their conservative opponents consider democracy incompatible with Islamic government in the form of the Khomeini's doctrine of theocracy (*velayat-e faqih*). The new democratic reading of Islam has been spread by the reformist press and resulted in the broad questioning of the legitimacy of the foundation of theocratic government as well as many of the clerical political and judiciary privileges.

**Shi`ite Reformation and the Conservative Ayatollahs**. The talk of a Shi`ite Reformation has spread far beyond the intellectual circles around the lay Islamic modernist, `Abdol-Karim Sorush, and the modernist cleric, Mohammad Mojtahed-Shabestari, and President Khatami himself has spread the dynamite notion that Islam is capable of more than one "reading" (*qera'at*). The conservative Ayatollahs, notably Mesbah-Yazdi, have reacted sharply by insisting on the categorical truth of their Islam and the need to defend it, if necessary, by violence.

Iranian Women in the Majles, the Universities and Seminaries. The highest number of votes in the 1996 and second highest in the 2000 elections for the highly contested seats for Tehran went to women. Women have been vocal in parliament and public life, pressing for all sorts of legal and administrative reform. The number of women entering universities has tripled in the last decade, and they now outnumber men in a number of fields, including medicine. Women have even found their way into institutions of higher education in the holy city of Qom, where they have their own seminary and recently went on strike to protest the inferior quality of the medical education they were offered in that city. Despite the rapid increase in the number of highly educated women, however, comparatively few can find employment by international standards, especially if they are married.

Can the Ayatollahs close down the reformist press indefinitely? The press is at the center of the power struggle between the reformist Sixth Majles, elected in 2000, and the conservative Ayatollahs and their followers who blame it for their poor showing in the popular elections of the previous three years. The clerics have used the courts to close down most of the reformist papers and try their editors, while the Participation Front majority in the Majles, whose newspaper is among the ones closed down, has vowed to change the press laws and fight the clerical abuse of judiciary power. Tension over the clampdown on the press escalated when Leader (the supreme jurist) Khamane`i stepped outside the Constitution and ordered the Majles to stop debating its press law in August.

References

Ahmad, Mumtaz. 1991 "Islamic Fundamentalism in South Asia: The Jamaati Islami and the Tablighi Jamaat," in M. Marty and R.S. Appleby, eds., *Fundamentalisms Comprehended*, University of Chicago Press.

Arjomand, Said A. 1986. "Social Change and Movements of Revitalization in Contemporary Islam," in James Beckford, ed., *New Religious Movements and Rapid Social Change*, Sage Publications.

_____. 1988. "Ideological Revolution in Shi`ism," in *Authority and Political Culture in Shi`ism*, Albany, NY: State University of New York Press.

_____. 1993. "Shi`ite Jurisprudence and Constitution-Making in the Islamic Republic of Iran," in M. Marty and R.S. Appleby, eds., *Fundamentalisms and the State. Remaking Polities, Economies, and Militance*, University of Chicago Press.

_____. 1995. "Unity and Diversity in Islamic Fundamentalism," in M. Marty and R.S. Appleby, eds., *Fundamentalisms Comprehended*, University of Chicago Press.

_____. 1996. "Religious Human Rights and the Principle of Legal Pluralism in the Middle East," in J. van der Vyver and J. Witte, eds., *Religious Human Rights in Global Perspective*, Vol. 2: *Legal Perspectives*, M. Nijhoff.

Barber, Benjamin R. 1995. *Jihad vs. McWorld*, New York: Random House.

Eickelman, Dale F. 1998. "Inside the Islamic Reformation," *Wilson Quarterly*, 22.1: 80 89.

Gellner, Ernest. 1994. *Conditions of Liberty. Civil Society and Its Rivals*. London: Hamish Hamilton.

Gibb, H.A.R. 1970. "The Heritage of Islam in the Modern World," *International Journal of Middle East Studies*, 1.1.

Huntington, Samuel P. 1996. *The Clash of Civilizations and the Remaking of World Order*, New York: Simon & Schuster.

Hunwick, J. 1996. "Sub-Saharan Africa and the Wider World of Islam: Historical and Comparative Perspectives," *Journal of Religion in Africa*, 26.3.

Jansen, Johannes J.G. 1986. *The Neglected Duty : The Creed of Sadat's Assassins and Islamic Resurgence in the Middle East*, New York : Macmillan.

Khatami, Mohammad. 1997. *Hope and Challenge. The Iranian President Speaks.* Binghamton, N.Y.: Institute of Global and Cultural Studies.

Marty, Martin and Appleby, R. Scott. 1995. "Introduction," *Fundamentalisms Comprehended*, University of Chicago Press.

Mayer, Ann E. 1994. "Universal versus Islamic Human Rights: A Clash of Cultures or a Clash of Constructs?" *Michigan Journal of International Law*, 15.2.

Mottahedeh, Roy P. 1993. "Toward an Islamic Theology of Toleration," in Tore Lindholm and Kari Vogt, eds., *Islamic Reform and Human Rights. Challenges and Rejoinders*, Copenhagen, Lund, Oslo, Abo/Turku.

Munson, Henry. 1988. *Islam and Revolution in the Middle East*, New Haven: Yale University Press.

Naipaul, V.S. 1981. *Among the Believers. An Islamic Journey*, New York: Knopf.

_____. 1998. *Beyond Belief. Islamic Excursions among the Converted Peoples*, New York: Random House.

Qutb, Sayyid. 1990. *Milestones*, A.Z. Hammad, tr., Indianapolis: American Trust Publication.

Robinson, Glenn E. 1998. "Defensive Democratization in Jordan," *International Journal of Middle East Studies*, 30.3.

Said, Edward W. 1979. *Orientalism*, New York: Vintage Books.

_____. 1981. *Covering Islam. How the Media and the Experts Determine How We See the Rest of the World*, New York: Pantheon Books.

V

Profiles in Pluralism:
Religion and Politics in Indonesia

Robert W. Hefner

In the first week of September 1999, the American public was treated to awful images of burning and killing in the former Portuguese territory of East Timor. Invaded by Indonesian forces at the end of 1975, the East Timorese had long resisted integration into their big brother neighbor. When offered the opportunity in August 1999 to decide their future, the East Timorese voted overwhelmingly in favor of independence. The Indonesian armed forces responded to this defiance by unleashing a wave of militia terror against native Timorese. In the weeks that followed, Western journalists showed great courage in reporting on the Timor violence. Their professionalism played a key role in shaping world opinion in such a manner as to bring a speedy resolution to the crisis.

Although the Western news media showed impressive acumen in reporting on East Timor, their insight into the other player in this conflict, Indonesia, was less confident. This reflected a major lacuna in Western public awareness generally, and American public awareness in particular. For of all the large countries in the world, Indonesia—the fourth most populous—is perhaps the least familiar to the American public.

Americans have a clear if sometimes simplistic idea of China, India, and Russia, but many have little idea of what Indonesia is like or even where it is. Those with any impression often associate it with Buddhism, beaches, and lush volcanic vistas. Indonesia once had a significant Buddhist population, and the stunning beauty of this archipelagic country in Southeast Asia is real enough. But far more significant for an understanding of the realities of modern Indonesia is the fact that it is the largest majority Muslim country in the world. Some 88 percent of Indonesia's 210 million people officially profess Islam. The others are a mix of Christians (nine percent), Hindus, Buddhists, and Confucians, with a healthy dose of indigenous mysticism running through local religious culture as a whole.

To identify Indonesia as predominantly Muslim only makes more daunting the task of understanding religion and politics there. If Indonesia evokes too little for Westerners, these days Islam tends to evoke too much: ready-made stereotypes of fanaticism and intolerance, and even anxieties about an imminent "clash of civilizations."[1] Reporters who visit Indonesia quickly learn that these harsh stereotypes fare poorly in the face of Muslim Indonesians' warmth and generosity. But some Westerners only conclude from this that Indonesians must not be very serious about their Islam. Sensitive to their own stereotypes and sobered by the difficulties of addressing big issues in short sound-bites, other reporters throw up their hands and choose simply to leave the question of Islam to the side in their reporting. The result is that religion has figured surprisingly little in contemporary coverage of culture and politics in Indonesia.

Like it or not, however, religion plays a vital part in Indonesian public affairs. Equally important, the Islamic tradition in Indonesia offers rich insights into this complex nation and its remarkable movement for a democratic and pluralist reformation. Muslims were at the forefront of the democratic movement that brought down the 32-year Suharto dictatorship in May 1998. In international Muslim circles, Indonesian Muslims have long been among the most vocal in insisting that the modern ideals of democracy, human rights, and constitutional governance are entirely consistent with their religion. Not all Indonesians are Muslim, of course, and, as the recent violence in East Timor and eastern Indonesia remind us, not all who are Muslim are democratic or tolerant. Nonetheless, no Muslim country better illustrates the great diversity and hope in today's Islamic world.

In what follows I want to sketch briefly the nature of religion in contemporary Indonesia, and explain how it came to be the way it is. I will then examine religion's role in recent public affairs, including the overthrow of Suharto in May 1998 and the continuing struggle for democracy and justice.

One of the things that first strikes visitors to Indonesia is its immense social and physical diversity. A vast archipelago equal in breadth to the United States, Indonesia is made up of some 12,000 islands inhabited by more than 300 ethnic groups.[2] Although most of the population is descended from people of Austronesian or (as they used to be called) Malayo-Polynesian ancestry, there is also a smaller Melanesian population living in the eastern portion of the country, as well as influential immigrant communities descended from long-resident Arabs, Indians, and, most important of all, Chinese. Indonesia's rich ethnic mosaic no doubt adds to the country's relative incomprehensibility to Americans.

Although as a nation Indonesia is young, the elements that comprise its

---

[1] I have in mind here especially Samuel P. Huntington's *The Clash of Civilizations and the Remaking of World Order* (New York: Simon & Schuster, 1996).

[2] In reality, however, the diversity is not quite so dizzying as it first appears. Two ethnic groups—the Javanese and the Sundanese—together account for almost two-thirds of Indonesia's population, and the five largest ethnic groups make up about 80 percent.

cultural heritage reach back far into premodern history. Six centuries ago, two-thirds of the archipelago was loosely united under a great Hindu-Buddhist kingdom known as Majapahit, the capital of which was located on Java. The remains of this empire's greatest temples still today figure among the architectural wonders of the ancient world. For 1,000 years prior to Majapahit, Hindu-Buddhist civilization provided a cultural *lingua franca* across this archipelago, much as Greco-Roman civilization had done in the Mediterranean world prior to Christianity. As also with Mediterranean civilization, however, the earlier tradition, in this case Hindu-Buddhism, was eventually displaced by a civilizational late-comer, in this case Islam.

Although Muslims had traded and traveled in the region since the 8th century, in the 14th and 15th centuries they began to win large numbers of local residents to their faith. The change occurred in part because the Indian merchants with whom archipelago peoples traded had changed from being predominantly Hindu to predominantly Muslim. (Two centuries earlier, the last of India's great kingdoms had been conquered by Muslim invaders.) This change in the religious background of the Indian traders brought with it a steady influx of Muslim preachers and teachers to the archipelago. It was these peaceful scholars and *mullahs*, not armies of conquering invaders, who brought about the gradual Islamization of the island territory.[3]

Although Hindus in Bali (a small island to the east of Java) and tribal peoples in the remote interior of the archipelago's larger islands retained their ancestral religions, most of the region's bustling coastal societies converted to Islam between the 15th and 18th centuries. During roughly the same period, European colonialism put the final pieces of the Indonesian religious puzzle in place. Portuguese and Spanish colonialists established small pockets of Christian settlement on remote islands in eastern Indonesia. Arriving after the Iberians, the Dutch launched an ambitious program of colonization in the 18th and 19th centuries. Fearing it might disrupt their economic programs, the Dutch forbade Christian proselytization in the Muslim heartlands of the archipelago. But they promoted missionization in the still tribal hinterlands of Sumatra, Kalimantan, and Sulawesi. The result was that, by the early 20th century, the map of religion in Indonesia looked largely like what it is today. The archipelago's populous heartlands were overwhelmingly Muslim, but its island and interior hinterlands had small populations of Christians and animists.[4]

As it became a civilizational tradition, Islam, like all the great world religions, developed several different cultural streams, of which Indonesian Islam

---

[3] On the coming of Islam to Indonesia, see Anthony Reid, *Southeast Asia in the Age of Commerce, 1450-1680*, Volume Two: *Expansion and Crisis* (New Haven: Yale University Press, 1993), pp. 132-86, and M.C. Ricklefs, *A History of Modern Indonesia Since c. 1300*, Second Edition (Stanford: Stanford University Press, 1993).

[4] On the shaping of Indonesia's contemporary religious mosaic, see my "Religion: Evolving Pluralism," in Donald K. Emmerson, ed., *Indonesia Beyond Suharto* (Armonk, NY: M.E. Sharpe, 1999), pp. 205-36.

is one of the most distinctive. Consistent with indigenous religions and with the Sufi (Muslim-mystical) traditions influential throughout the Muslim world at the time, the Islam introduced to Indonesia in the early modern period was more deeply mystical than it was legalistic. As with orthodox Judaism, Islam is a religion of commandment and law, and its central religious officials are not priests or ministers but jurists (*ulama*) trained in the holy Qur'an and its associated legal commentaries. As also with Judaism, however, there has long been a tension in Muslim civilization between those who see ethics and law as the soul of their religion and those inclined to believe that mysticism and spiritual discipline are what is most really real. In the Indonesian case, it was mystical Islam, not law, that became the central element in the local practice of Islam. This spiritual heritage was to be challenged in the nineteenth and twentieth centuries by movements of Islamic reform emanating from the Middle East. Like Protestantism in Reformation Europe, these demanded a return to scripture and an unembellished spirituality. Although reformist Islam succeeded in making a place for itself in Indonesian culture, Muslim society as a whole still today shows the visible imprint of the mystical and tolerant Islam of the earlier period.[5]

Another thing giving Muslim traditions in this country a distinctive face is that, even as Islamic religious ideals took hold, pre-existing traditions in the arts, medicine, magic, gender ideals, and government were carried over into the emerging civilization. The result is that still today even the most deeply Islamized cultures in the archipelago have a hue different from that of the Muslim Middle East. In gender and sexuality, for example, the female veiling and seclusion so common in the Middle East were historically rare in Indonesia. (Among some strict reformists veiling has in recent years become common, but even here the practice is charged with meanings different from those typical in the Middle East.) Visitors to Indonesia are often struck by the conspicuousness of women in the marketplace and the ease with which women move about in villages and towns.

Similarly, travelers to Java—the most populous of Indonesia's islands, where more than 50 percent of Indonesians live—are often surprised to see that the art forms most esteemed in this Muslim society are those like shadow puppetry (*wayang kulit*) and traditional theater (*wayang wong*), which base their story line on narratives created in Java's Hindu past. Although fewer than one percent of Javanese are today Hindu, the great majority are familiar with and enjoy the Indonesianized Hindu deities who figure in these classical art forms. Cultural blending like this irritates the small minority of Muslims who regard as heretical any cultural tradition not directly based on the model of the

---

[5]   For an interpretation of this tension in Javanese religion and politics, see Mark R. Woodward, *Islam in Java: Normative Piety and Mysticism in the Sultanate of Yogyakarta* (Tucson: University of Arizona Press, 1989). For a classic but somewhat dated overview of the same tension, see Clifford Geertz, *The Religion of Java* (New York: Free Press, 1960).

Prophet Muhammad. For most Indonesian Muslims, however, such cultural traditions are regarded not as contrary to Islam, but as demonstrations of the fact that one can be Muslim without necessarily embracing all of the cultural habits of the Arab Middle East.

Examples like these illustrate something even more distinctive about Indonesia: Religious culture here has always been deeply plural. Lacking a centralized church or clerical hierarchy, the Muslim world has always shown a surprising measure of religious diversity by comparison with, say, premodern Europe or China. In the case of Indonesia, this pluralist disposition was taken even further as a result of the archipelago's ethnic diversity and political fragmentation. Although Javanese, Sundanese, and Minangkabau might all be Muslim, they were all aware that Islam had varied cultural expressions. Similarly, after the collapse of last Hindu empire around 1400, Indonesia had never been united until the Dutch consolidated their archipelagan empire at the beginning of the 20th century. After Hindu Majapahit, political organization around the Muslim archipelago resembled not so much the centralized imperial structures of China, Rome, or the Middle East, as the "pluricentric" political order of early modern Western Europe.[6] There was a host of small, competing political systems, among which movement was easy. For reasons too complicated to detail here, competition among states in this region did not create pressures for democratization as sustained as those in Western Europe. But it did insure that ethnic and religious culture remained diverse in its expression, and ordinary people developed the habit of tolerating different peoples and customs.

In recent years, Western political scientists have come to recognize that a peaceful and democratic politics depends not just on formal elections and constitutions, but on a "social capital" of traditions and organizations through which ordinary people learn "habits of the heart" consistent with democratic politics: popular participation, tolerance of differing opinions and lifestyles, and collaboration in projects that enhance the common good.[7] In Indonesia, one of the most distinctive sources of such social capital lay in the varied ways in which Islam and ethnic custom were practiced. From early on, Indonesians developed the eminently modern habit of recognizing their commonality across cultural differences.

One interesting consequence of this precedent was that, in the twentieth

---

[6] I discuss the legacy of political pluricentrism for modern Indonesian Islam in my, *Civil Islam: Muslims and Democratization in Indonesia* (Princeton: Princeton University Press, 2000), Chapter 2; cf. Reid, *Southeast Asia*, pp. 202-66. The contrast with Western Europe that I have in mind is best captured in John A. Hall, "In Search of Civil Society," in Hall, ed., *Civil Society: Theory, History, Comparison* (Cambridge, UK: Polity Press, 1995), pp. 1-31.

[7] The single most influential work in this genre is Robert D. Putnam's *Making Democracy Work: Civic Traditions in Modern Italy* (Princeton: Princeton University Press, 1993). For a collection that addresses similar issues in a Middle Eastern setting, see Augustus Richard Norton, *Civil Society in the Middle* East, Vol. 1 (Leiden: E.J. Brill, 1995).

century, the great majority of Indonesian Muslims found it easy to rally to the ideals of democratic and multiethnic nationalism. Whereas modern European societies have been plagued by a recurring tendency to construct nationalism on the basis of exclusive or even racist ethnic prototypes—Germans but not Poles in a German nation, Serbs but not Croats in a free Serbia, Christians but not Jews (or Muslims) in any number of countries—the central stream in Indonesian nationalism has from the beginning been inclusive, embracing people of all ethnic backgrounds *and* all religions. There has been a run on this legacy in recent years, not least by the Suharto dictatorship that ruled Indonesia from 1966 to 1998. But Indonesia's multiethnic and multireligious nationalism remains one of the strongest supports for Indonesian democracy to this day.

Although political analysts in recent years have recognized that democracy depends on more than the formal institutions of government, they have also emphasized that positive precedents in society can be wasted or wrecked by ruthless rulers or unhealthy political rivalries. Political cultures are by their very nature heterogeneous, carrying varied potentialities within, and historical events can take these latencies in widely varying directions. In the case of Indonesia, there was no better illustration of this problem than the long-reigning "New Order" government of President M. Suharto. Through his ruthless habit of playing different religious groups against each other, Suharto did great damage to Indonesia's tradition of pluralism and tolerance. However, he also unwittingly accelerated the development of a democratic opposition that eventually toppled his regime and strengthened the movement for a democratic and pluralist Islam.

Suharto came to power after the overthrow in 1966 of the first of Indonesia's presidents, Achmad Sukarno. Sukarno led Indonesia from its declaration of independence in 1945 up through his government's collapse in March 1966. Raised in a nominally Muslim family, Sukarno became an ardent proponent of socialism and secular nationalism in his youth. As Indonesia's first president, he tried to unite the nation by forging an unwieldy alliance among the country's major political streams: nationalists, Muslims, and communists. Although this strategy worked well enough for a few years, in the end it gave rise to fierce competition and, ultimately, catastrophic violence.

In the final years of Sukarno's rule in the early 1960s, the Communist Party managed to transform itself into the largest of the country's political parties. This success only deepened the animosity of the Muslim parties, which feared that the rise of the communists would bring about the demise of Islam. The ascent of the communists also antagonized the country's single most powerful organization, the armed forces. The army had a long and officially approved history of involvement in political affairs, under a policy known in the Suharto era as the "two functions" (*dwifungsi*). As communist power increased, then, the armed forces threw themselves into a campaign of anti-communist mobilization. When in the early 1960s the communists launched a massive campaign to organize the rural poor, the military responded by organizing anticommunist militias, especially among conservative Muslims. (In this, we are reminded that the East Timorese militias unleashed by the Indonesian military in 1999 have a clear historical precedent.) As the economy went into a tailspin during 1964-1965, the competition degenerated into bitter violence.[8]

On September 30, 1965, left-wing junior officers in Jakarta attempted to break the country's political impasse by launching a coup against the conservative military command. The rebel effort collapsed in just two days, but it provided the senior military leadership with a pretext to strike at the Communist Party. Over the next six months, the army mobilized Muslims, anticommunist nationalists, Hindus (in Bali), and others to launch fierce attacks on the Communist Party, which the army blamed for the junior officers' coup. A half million people died in the bloodbath; two million more were imprisoned. When the violence was over, little remained of Indonesia's parliamentary order, and the Communist Party—previously the largest in the non-communist world—lay in ruins.

It was out of this maelstrom of violence that the Suharto regime emerged. The military relied heavily on Muslim militias in the anticommunist campaign, and, as a result, Muslim leaders at first expected to be rewarded with early elections (which, with the communists now gone, they were confident they could win) and appointments to key governmental posts. From early on, however, the military-dominated government made clear that it had no intention of giving civilian organizations any real power. Suharto and the military quickly imposed strict controls on Muslim and all other organizations. The regime also delayed the country's elections until 1971, so as to give it time to organize its own party. At the same time, it maintained the ban on what had once been the most popular of Muslim parties, Masyumi (banned by Sukarno in 1960); fused the four remaining Muslim parties into a single corporatist structure; and interfered in the selection of leaders for all political parties.

Christians and secular nationalists were subject to these same restrictions. However, with the destruction of the political left and the discrediting of the nationalists in 1965-1966, it was Muslim organizations that felt the brunt of regime controls. Western scholars reflecting on the early New Order once attributed these actions to Suharto's alleged "Javanist" or *abangan*[9] biases.

---

[8]   The best study of the Communist Party's tactics during this time is Rex Mortimer's *Indonesian Communism under Sukarno: Ideology and Politics, 1959-1965* (Ithaca: Cornell University Press, 1974).

[9]   *Abangan* is a Javanese term that literally means "red." But in Javanese tradition the term is posed in opposition to people of strict Islamic persuasion, the "whites" (*putihan*) or *santri* (people who have received formal Islamic education).

Javanists or *abangan* are ethnic Javanese who nominally identify as Muslim but, like many Catholics in Europe and Latin America, are otherwise lax in their devotional duties. During the Sukarno era, they provided the bulk of support for the nationalists and communists in their rivalry with Muslim parties. Suharto's Javanist convictions, of course, had little to do with nationalist or leftist sympathies; his spiritual interest lay in an elitist Javanism that employed magic and mysticism for the purpose of personal power.

In retrospect, then, it is clear that Suharto's early opposition to Muslim parties had less to do with his alleged Javanist sympathies than with his ruthless determination to increase his own power and eliminate all rivals. During the first years of his rule, Suharto not only imposed tight controls on Muslim social organizations but also banned more than 100 Javanist mystical sects he viewed as left wing. In the 1980s, when Indonesia experienced an historically unprecedented Islamic resurgence, the president quickly changed course and presented himself as a great patron of Muslims. He invited an Islamic preacher from the armed forces to train him in Islamic devotion, greetings, and scripture. Between 1988 and 1993, Suharto's regime approved the founding of the first Islamic bank; expanded the authority of Islamic courts; lifted the prohibition on the Islamic veil (*jilbab*, *hijab*) in schools; supported the founding of an Islamic newspaper; abolished the state-run sports lottery; increased Muslim programming on television; provided more funds to mosques and Muslim schools; and replaced the Catholic head of the armed forces with generals more sympathetic to Islam.[10]

Why the change? In part, we know, the president took these actions because he was being challenged by high-ranking figures in the armed forces, especially the armed forces' chief of staff, Benny Moerdani. Moerdani was the most powerful of the generals ever to serve under Suharto. A strict disciplinarian and opponent of democratic reform, he was also one of the architects of the 1975 invasion of East Timor. Ironically in light of the awful loss of life in that Catholic territory, Moerdani also happens to have been a Catholic. Indeed some political observers have long suspected that Suharto tolerated Moerdani's growing influence because the president recognized that, as a Catholic, Moerdani would never be able to challenge Suharto's rule.

In the late 1980s, however, the Catholic general had the audacity to meet privately with the president and urge him to rein in his children. The 1980s were a time when Suharto's offspring came of age and began to demand a lion's share of the contracts awarded for big state projects and joint ventures with

---

[10]   On the broader dynamics of the president's actions, see my, "Islam and Nation in the Post-Suharto Era," in Adam Schwarz and Jonathan Paris, *The Politics of Post-Suharto Indonesia* (New York: Council of Foreign Relations, 1999), pp. 40-72. On the president's uneasy relationship with the armed forces during this period, see Takashi Shirashi's essay in the same volume, "The Indonesian Military in Politics," pp. 73-86.

foreign firms.[11] Earlier, during the first years of the New Order, there had been an unwritten rule that such contracts were to be awarded to senior retirees from the armed forces. As the Suharto children came of age, however, the president violated this understanding and began to channel the most lucrative contracts to his children and his Chinese-Indonesian business partners.[12] These actions caused great resentment in military circles. As armed forces commander, Moerdani took it upon himself to convey the military's disquiet to the president. Suharto responded to these gentle urgings by removing Moerdani from command and launching a program of "de-Moerdanization" in the officer corps as a whole. Around this same time, Suharto began his courtship of conservative Muslims.

According to cabinet officials that I had the opportunity to interview during these years, the rivalry with the military was not the only consideration figuring in Suharto's putative Islamic turn. The president was also aware of the enormous scale of the Islamic revival that had swept the country in the 1980s. The revival was in part the unintentional consequence of New Order policies. Hoping to prevent a communist revival, the regime in 1967 had outlawed atheism, required all citizens to profess one of five recognized religions (Islam, Protestantism, Catholicism, Hinduism, or Buddhism), and made religious education mandatory from elementary school through university. Since Javanism and mysticism were not among the available options for students, this policy forced the offspring of nominal Muslims to take their religion more seriously than their parents ever had. In the late 1960s, the government ministries of religion and the interior also launched programs of religious "building up" (*pembinaan*) in former communist strongholds and other regions deemed lax in their piety. The regime also promoted the construction of mosques and prayer houses across the country, doubling their number in the densely populated provinces of East and Central Java in just ten years.[13]

There were broader societal influences on the Islamic resurgence as well. The 1970s and 1980s were a time of religious revitalization in most of the Muslim world. The movement was in part prompted by the Muslim public's disappointment over the inability of secular nationalist parties to make good on their promises of economic prosperity and political

---

[11]   On Suharto's economic policies in the early New Order, see Richard Robison, *Indonesia: The Rise of Capital* (North Sydney, Australia: Allen & Unwin, 1986).

[12]   On Suharto's involvement in the economy, see John Bresnan, *Managing Indonesia: Managing the Modern Political Economy* (New York: Columbia University Press, 1993), and Adam Schwarz, *A Nation in Waiting: Indonesia's Search for Stability* (Boulder: Westview, 2000), pp. 132-61.

[13]   On religious policy in the early New Order, see my, "Islamization and Democratization in Indonesia," in Hefner and Patricia Horvatich, eds., *Islam in an Era of Nation-States: Politics and Religious Renewal in Muslim Southeast Asia* (Honolulu: University of Hawaii Press, 1997), pp. 75-127.

progress.[14] But the resurgence also reflected a basic change in Muslim culture and social organization. Muslim society in the 1950s and 1960s was deeply affected by the expansion of mass education, which made the bulk of the population literate for the first time in world history.[15] In the case of Indonesia, between 1965 and the early 1990s, the percentage of young adults with basic literacy skills skyrocketed from 40 percent to 90 percent.[16] The percentage rise in the number of high school graduates was equally dramatic, going from four percent in 1970 to more than 30 percent in the 1990s.[17] With literacy one saw a spectacular increase in the market for inexpensive and accessible religious publications for ordinary Muslims. Ordinary people began to show an interest in defining their religion in their own terms.

These developments readied the ground for a far-reaching change in Muslim knowledge and authority in the 1970s. Education brought into existence a new generation of Muslim activists and intellectuals who challenged the monopoly of religious authority long enjoyed by the classically trained specialists of Islamic knowledge, the *ulama*. Whereas *ulama* are graduates of classical Muslim schools, most of the new intellectuals typically came from secular universities. While the *ulama* are masters of esoteric commentaries on religion and law, the new Muslim intellectuals tend to be eclectic in their interests and training. They apply their knowledge of Islam not just to the classical concerns of Muslim jurisprudence but to issues affecting the lives of ordinary Muslims: changing sex roles, the anomie of urban life, economic hardship, corruption, and political injustice.[18]

In the case of Indonesia, the new intellectuals' interest in politics was also influenced by the New Order's tight controls on all other forms of

---

[14] The religious challenge to secular nationalism was not unique to the Muslim world, of course. For a comparative analysis, see Mark Juergensmeyer, *The New Cold War? Religious Nationalism Confronts the Secular State* (Berkeley: University of California Press, 1993). For an Indian example, see Peter van der Veer, *Religious Nationalism: Hindus and Muslims in India* (Berkeley: University of California Press, 1994).

[15] On the political impact of mass education and new religious media, see Dale F. Eickelman and James Piscatori, *Muslim Politics* (Princeton: Princeton University Press, 1996), and Dale F. Eickelman and Jon W. Anderson, *New Media in the Muslim World: The Emerging Public Sphere* (Bloomington: University of Indiana Press, 1999). For a comparative analysis of Muslim politics during the same period, see John L. Esposito and John O. Voll, *Islam and Democracy* (New York: Oxford University Press, 1996).

[16] Gavin W. Jones and Chris Manning, "Labour Force and Employment during the 1980s," in Anne Booth, ed., *The Oil Boom and After: Indonesian Economic Policy and Performance in the Soeharto Era*, (Kuala Lumpur: Oxford University Press, 1992), pp. 363-410.

[17] Terence H. Hull and Gavin W. Jones, "Demographic Perspectives," in Hal Hill, ed., *Indonesia's New Order: The Dynamics of Socio-Economic Transformation*, (Honolulu: University of Hawaii Press, 1994), pp. 123-78.

[18] On the new Muslim intellectuals in a different country, see Michael E. Meeker, "The New Muslim Intellectuals in the Republic of Turkey," in Richard Tapper, ed., *Islam in Modern Turkey: Religion, Politics, and Literature in a Secular State* (London: I.B. Tauris, 1991), pp. 189-219.

political activity. As the journalist and author Adam Schwarz has observed,[19] many Indonesians saw Islam "as a safe alternative to the heavily circumscribed political structure." Mosques and Islamic schools offered some of the few arenas for open discussion of vital public issues. Anxious not to invite Muslim resentment, the government was reluctant to take action against these activities except where they directly challenged the regime. In most other spheres of public life, meanwhile, the regime applied ever more strict political controls. In 1974, it cracked down on the national press. In 1978 it imposed draconian restrictions on campus political activity. Between 1983 and 1985, the government required religious and other mass organizations to incorporate the state ideology (known as the *Pancasila* or "five principles") into their organizational charters; those that opted not to do so were banned. Faced with this repression, many public-spirited people channeled their energies out of politics and into religion.

As the Islamic revival progressed, Suharto launched a series of preemptive strikes intended to create the impression that he had changed and was now a great patron of Islam. Consistent with his longstanding strategy of divide and conquer, however, Suharto made clear from the start that the Muslims he sought to support were conservative Muslims willing to trade patronage favors for help in containing the democratic opposition. In line with this strategy, in the early 1990s presidential aides and Muslim conservatives alike began to criticize supporters of human rights and democracy as "Westernizers." Suhartoists and conservative Islamists also portrayed the pro-democracy movement, which included many pious Muslims in its ranks, as Christian and secularist. Not coincidentally, it was around this same time that Suharto's spokespersons began to respond to Western criticisms on East Timor by saying the accusations were really motivated by the desire of Christians and Jews to humiliate Indonesia because it is a majority-Muslim country. Never before had the Muslim card been played in so direct and provocative a manner. But this was just the beginning of Suharto's "Islamic" turn.

Suharto's appeals to Muslim leaders were always highly selective. When he began his courtship in the late 1980s, the first target of his affections was the executive chairman of the country's largest Muslim organization, Abdurrahman Wahid of the Nahdlatul Ulama (NU). Elected president of Indonesia in October 1998 (to the astonishment of Suhartoist conservatives), Wahid is one of the most intriguingly original figures in the whole Muslim world. Descended from a distinguished family of Javanese *ulama*, Wahid was educated in Egypt and Iraq in the 1960s and 1970s. Sent to study Islamic law at the conservative Al-Azhar University in Cairo, he quickly grew restless and dedicated much of his attention not to the study of religious law but to Western sociology, democratic theory, German classical music, and French

---

[19] Schwarz, *A Nation in Waiting*, p. 164.

cinema. Upon his return to Indonesia in the 1970s, he tried briefly to return
to teaching and preaching, but soon found himself drawn to the high cultural
life of Indonesia's capital. In the late 1970s, he shocked his fellow *ulama* by
twice acting as chairperson for a program most of them regarded as unaccept-
ably risqué, the Jakarta film festival.

Elected chairman of NU in 1984, Wahid worked over the next six years to
modernize his organization, transforming it from a simple vehicle of *ulama*
representation into an agent of grassroots development and pluralist democracy. He and others in the pro-democracy wing of the Muslim community were
opposed to all efforts to create an Islamic state or otherwise devalue the citizenship rights of non-Muslims. They sought to build on local traditions of pluralism, gender equity, and civil participation so that Muslims could work with
rather than against the forces of democratization.

As leader of the NU, it was inevitable that Wahid would attract Suharto's
attention. In 1988, Suharto appointed Wahid to the People's Consultative
Assembly, a largely ceremonial body that every five years puts the final stamp
on the election of the president and outlines the basic goals of government policy. Around the same time, Suharto also began to provide new business contracts to NU firms. By 1990, however, Suharto realized that Wahid was interested in social justice and democracy, not just patronage, and so he began to
withhold favors from the NU leader. In 1993 and 1994, Suharto went further,
interfering directly in NU politics in an attempt to remove Wahid from the
executive leadership. The president's meddling so irritated the organization's
ulama that they re-elected Wahid.[20] Determined to stick to his pro-democracy course, in 1995 and 1996 Wahid began to speak openly of an alliance with
the leader of the secular nationalist Democratic Party, Megawati Sukarnoputri,
the daughter of the country's first president. In a secret report drafted in a
regime think tank, the president's advisors warned that, if the alliance came to
fruition, it might well topple Suharto.

Angered by Wahid's defiance, Suharto's advisors launched a series of initiatives designed to discredit Wahid and drive Megawati from the leadership of
the Democratic Party. Pro-Suharto Muslims spread rumors that Wahid didn't
pray, was a socialist, and was in the hire of wealthy Chinese Indonesians. The
regime recruited a minor NU businessman to organize a dissident executive
board for the Muslim organization, challenging Wahid's leadership. Despite
these efforts, however, the organization held firm and Wahid retained his
chairmanship of NU.

As it became clear that the effort to oust Wahid was failing, the regime
changed tack and turned its attention to the Democratic Party's Megawati.

---

[20]   For an English-language overview of Wahid and NU during this period, see Greg Barton and
Greg Fealy, eds., *Nahdlatul Ulama, Traditional Islam and Modernity in Indonesia* (Clayton,
Australia: Monash Asia Institute, 1996). On NU's early history and contemporary evolution,
see Andrée Feillard, *Islam et Armée dans l'Indonésie Contemporaine* (Paris: L'Harmattan, 1995).

During 1994 and 1995, regime propagandists launched a blistering propaganda campaign portraying Megawati as secularist and anti-Islamic; they also claimed that Megawati was allowing the party to be taken over by Christians and communists. Shortly thereafter, the regime also accused her husband, Taufik Kiemas, of having collaborated with the Communist Party in the 1960s. When these tactics only increased public sympathy for the embattled Megawati, Suharto's aides took a cue from the earlier effort against Wahid and arranged the establishment of a rival executive board. The board organized a national congress in June 1996 and promptly expelled Megawati from the party leadership. When Megawati's supporters continued to defy Suharto's proxies, the president upped the ante. On July 27, 1996, Suhartoist officers hired street criminals and out-of-uniform soldiers to evict Megawati's supporters from the Democratic Party's national headquarters. Several of Megawati supporters died in the attack. With great fanfare, the regime also arrested several supporters of the Democratic Party, claiming the men were actually communist agents attempting a take over of the party.

Although it succeeded in toppling Megawati, the government was still unable to contain Wahid. As leader of the 32-million-strong NU, Wahid could not be easily portrayed as a Christian or a communist, and, with his many Muslim supporters, any effort to oust him by force was risky. In October 1996, however, an incident occurred that many observers felt reflected the regime's new strategy against the NU leader. Under highly suspicious circumstances, a riot broke out in an area long regarded as a stronghold of Wahid's Nahdlatul Ulama, the town of Situbondo in East Java. By the standards of the violence to come, this was only a small incident; five people died. But the targets of the violence sent a chill down the spine of Indonesia's democratic activists. Chinese stores were burned and 25 Christian churches were destroyed. Now, it seemed, the regime was not only playing the Muslim card but was also actively promoting anti-Christian and anti-Chinese hatred. As Wahid reported to me in early 1997, his intelligence advisors informed him that the violence had been instigated by secret regime operatives intent on discrediting him by demonstrating that he could not control his membership. The riot was also intended to show that Wahid's vision of a tolerant Islam had little support among his rank-and-file.

In the months to come, there were other acts of violence, many of which had signatures as suspicious as Situbondo. In East Java, for example, there were a series of "ninja" killings in 1997 and then again in 1998, in which burly men in black nylon outfits made nighttime excursions into the countryside to target hapless victims for torture, execution, and dismemberment. Some 150 individuals died in this manner. When this violence was reported in the Western media, including the *New York Times* in August of 1998, it was often portrayed as a kind of mad frenzy motivated by Javanese superstitions.

Abdurrahman Wahid and his advisors, however, had no such illusions about the cause of the killings. Those targeted for execution, Wahid pointed out, came from two backgrounds. Some were nominal Muslims or *abangan*, often from families that had been communists in the 1960s. According to conventional understandings in Java, these people were likely supporters of Megawati's Democratic Party. The other victims of the violence were local preachers and scholars associated with Abdurrahman Wahid's NU. At the sites of many of the killings investigators found leaflets explaining that the victim had been targeted because he or she came from the opposing religious community. Spokespersons for Suharto echoed this charge, claiming that the killings were perpetrated by the children of communists intent on taking revenge on NU for that organization's complicity in the 1965 killings. Conversely, it was claimed, NU supporters killed nominal or abangan Muslims, allegedly blaming them for killing Muslim scholars. Consistent with Wahid's information, however, independent investigators argued that the killings were the work of regime operatives, intent on scuttling the alliance between Megawati's Democratic Party and Wahid's NU by creating tensions between NU and nominal (*abangan*) Muslims.

In the face of this violence, as well as a rash of church burnings and attacks on Chinese during late 1997 and 1998, Wahid and the NU leadership mobilized a network of activists to guard against violence. In East Java, NU had its youth affiliates organize peace patrols around Christian Churches and Chinese stores. The leadership provided some of these observers with cellular phones, an extremely expensive item in Indonesia. Despite repeated acts of provocation, then, the province held firm and there were no outbreaks of sectarian violence. Muslim civil society had challenged and neutralized regime terror.

Unfortunately, rather than pulling back from provocations of this kind, regime operatives escalated their violence during the final months of the Suharto regime in 1998, as the economy spiraled out of control and the anti-Suharto campaign intensified. In November 1997, the regime sponsored the publication of "The Conspiracy to Overthrow Suharto," a 50-page document which it circulated to conservative Muslim circles in early 1998. The document's most startling claim concerned the economic crisis afflicting Indonesia. The crisis is not the result of Suharto's mismanagement, crony capitalism, or corruption, the document explained, but of an international conspiracy of Jews, the American CIA, the Vatican, and Chinese-Indonesians against Suharto *because he is a Muslim and Indonesia is a majority Muslim country*. The pro-democracy movement was denounced in similar terms as product of a foreign conspiracy against the president, the nation, the military, and Islam. The regime's repressive machinery seemed to be revving up for another attack.

In January 1998, the target of this new round of regime propaganda became clearer. At the end of that month, Suharto aides accused a conservative Chinese businessman (Sofyan Wanandi) of providing funds to a small leftwing group for a bombing campaign to bring Suharto down. Such an alliance between a wealthy conglomerate owner and a small band of New Left idealists was ridiculously improbable, but the regime's intent was all-too apparent. A few weeks earlier, this Chinese man, once one of Suharto's strongest supporters, had gone public with his opposition to the president's defiance of IMF demands for economic reform. Suharto's attack on Wenandi and other Chinese businessmen was intended to deflect the growing opposition to his rule by suggesting that the economic crisis was not Suharto's fault, but had been created by a hateful cabal of Chinese, Christians, and pro-democracy activists intent on toppling Suharto because he was Muslim.

Shortly afterwards, as if on cue, hard-line ministers in the cabinet as well as police and bureaucrats in the provinces began to make not-so-veiled threats against Chinese shopowners. In February and March 1998, as food prices escalated wildly, government spokespersons claimed that the inflation was the result not of presidential mismanagement but of hoarding by Chinese shopkeepers. Pro-military conservatives in the Muslim community echoed this charge. The leadership of KISDI, a small pro-Suharto and pro-military Muslim organization, called openly for a campaign against all "rats" and "traitors" to the nation. Everyone understood what this meant. The grounds for an assault on Chinese and other opponents of the regime were being readied.

In the end, we know, the gauntlet was indeed thrown down, and with stunning effect. On the night of May 14-15, 1998, in the aftermath of an army sniper execution of four student demonstrators, urban riots broke out across Indonesia. About 2,000 people died in the subsequent violence. Thousands of Chinese stores were also destroyed and portions of many big cities were burned out. Although at first the mayhem seemed like the spontaneous product of protestor outrage, we now know that the riots were engineered by hard-line members of the military. Their plan was to create a political crisis so severe that Suharto would declare a state of emergency, hand special powers over to hard-line officers, and arrest and liquidate the democratic opposition.

Some of the worst violence at this time took place in Jakarta. In addition to 1,200 deaths there, more than 160 Chinese-Indonesian women were hunted down and raped in their stores, offices, and homes by teams of well-organized thugs intent on terrorizing Indonesian Chinese. For all of its wanton brutality, however, this desperate effort to save Suharto backfired. Muslims and non-Muslims alike rejected the vile appeals to ethno-religious hatred. One cannot emphasize too strongly that Muslim leaders, in particular, acted with great courage, mobilizing all the more vigorously against Suharto because they recognized his willingness to abuse their religion for the purpose of maintaining power. On May 21, 1998, under pressure from the pro-democracy movement, segments of the military, and the Muslim leadership, President Suharto stepped down.

Unfortunately, Indonesia's anguish did not end with this democratic triumph. Over the months that followed other incidents revealed that, although

Suharto was gone, many of his supporters were still in power. In late 1998 and early 1999, hard-line Muslims denounced those calling for investigations of the May rapes and killings, claiming that those making such demands were Christians and secularists intent on discrediting Muslims, the military, and Indonesia. In November 1998, an 18-year-old old rape counselor of Chinese ethnicity was herself found raped and murdered days before she was to head off to the U.S. to testify before Congress about the May violence. Abdurrahman Wahid was also the target of violent threats during this time because of statements he made calling for probes into the violence. These and other incidents showed a similar pattern of *ancien régime* manipulation of conservative Islamist sensibilities. Although the violence diminished prior to the elections of June 1999 and then again prior Wahid's surprise election to the presidency in October 1999, it started up again just after Wahid took office. Indeed, shortly after Wahid's inauguration, *ninja* killings began again in East Java.

Some of the worst violence in the past year, however, has taken place in the Maluku islands in the far northeastern corner of the Indonesian archipelago. This is a region where, unlike the rest of the country, Christians and Muslims live alongside each other in almost equal numbers. For most of history they have lived in peace but since January 1999 the region has been plagued by one bloody incident after another. In January 2000, hundreds of people were massacred in the worst outbreak of killing thus far. As in East Java in 1997 and 1998, the violence has been accompanied by propaganda that seeks to blame people from one religious community for violence against the other. Despite this disinformation, it is widely believed that rogue elements of the armed forces have provoked the violence. Their purpose, it is said, is to distract attention from demands for an investigation into human rights abuses by Suharto and the military.

Unlike events in East Java a year earlier, the violence in Maluku has now sunk its roots into society and acquired a momentum all its own. Each side in the conflict has been mysteriously supplied with firearms, and well-coordinated leafleting keeps hateful propaganda in the air. Earlier, in East Java, efforts like these failed because of the courageous efforts of the NU leadership under Wahid. In the face of church burnings and the Ninja killings, the Muslim leadership mobilized its resources and succeeded in preventing sectarian violence. In Maluku, however, there is no NU or any other well-established non-state organization able to contain the violence or counteract the lies. The absence of civic organizations has proved a critical vulnerability and undercut efforts to douse sectarian fires. As Wahid has made clear (including in remarks to me in late November 1999), he believes hard-line elements of the *ancien régime* are using the violence in order to slow the course of democratic reform. He is convinced the violence is also intended to show that only a non-civilian hand can effectively govern Indonesia.

Since his election to the presidency in October 1999, Wahid, the great survivor of Suharto repression, has shown himself to be a brilliant reformer and tactician. Despite repeated warnings of an imminent military coup, he has made great headway in his efforts to replace hard-line elements of the military with supporters of reform. Although the political crisis is far from over, there are signs that he may yet achieve something just short of a democratic miracle.

As this overview indicates, there is little in the history discussed here of the uniform and anti-democratic "Muslim politics" of which some Western observers have spoken in recent years. Certainly Indonesia's turmoil has not created a seamless Muslim consensus on the virtues of pluralist democracy. And a small minority of Muslims continues to claim that the ideals of modern democracy and citizenship are contrary to Islam.

But the more striking lesson is that Suharto's abuses convinced the majority of Muslim leaders that what they most need is a democratic, law-abiding, and self-limiting state. From the perspective of the larger Muslim world, this change in political culture is a remarkable event. The largest majority-Muslim society in the world now has the strongest Muslim-led democracy movement. Indonesian Muslims showed great courage in standing up to a violent dictatorship; they are right to feel that their actions demonstrate that Islam and democracy are compatible.

More generally, the Indonesian example reminds us that there is no single Muslim politics, least of all of the austerely authoritarian sort promoted by some conservative Muslims in the Middle East and Africa. Over the past 15 years, many of us in the West have failed to notice that a quiet, peaceful revolution has begun in parts of the Muslim world.[21] Overshadowed by the Islamic revolution in Iran and the awful violence in Algeria and Afghanistan, the Muslim world has seen the emergence of a new class of intellectuals and activists committed to the idea that Muslims can work with and for pluralist democracy. Indeed, as here in Indonesia, some Muslims speak not only of democracy's *compatibility* with their religion, but of its *necessity*. In a world of modern states vastly more powerful than those of premodern times, these thinkers argue, Muslim leaders must keep a respectful distance from state elites. They must do so, they say, *not* so as to enforce a liberal "separation of religion and state" but to guarantee that high religious ideals are not subordinated to the low interests of despots and thugs. In the past few years we have even begun to hear Muslim leaders argue that politics in their countries must be based on a healthy civil society that counterbalances state power, rather than increasing it.

---

[21] For a selection of writings from this emerging tradition, see Charles Kurzman, *Liberal Islam: A Sourcebook* (New York: Oxford University Press, 1998). For essays addressing a similar problem from the perspective of Islamic law, see Tore Lindholm and Kari Vogt, *Islamic Law Reform and Human Rights: Challenges and Rejoinders* (Copenhagen: Nordic Human Rights Publications, 1993).

In all this, the lessons of Indonesia have implications well beyond this Southeast Asian nation. The Muslim democrats among whom I have worked for more than a decade are themselves firmly convinced of this fact. They hope that their experience provides a positive testimony to Muslims everywhere on Islam and democracy. Time and time again, however, these Muslims also expressed the hope that the Indonesian example will catch the attention of Westerners skeptical of the possibility of a democratic Islam. As a now deceased Muslim activist and friend of mine, Aswab Mahasin, once put it, "I would hope Westerners come to recognize in us our common humanity, as well as the common challenges we moderns face. We're all God's creatures in this world, and though we have traveled different roads we can reach similar destinations, democratic ones." In an age when relativist cynicism is easy, I'd like to think Aswab's simple Muslim humanism captures the truth of our modern situation precisely.

Issues to Keep an Eye on

The Problem of the Parapolitical. One of the most unfortunate legacies of the Suharto era was the regime's reliance on parapolitical organizations and extralegal violence to achieve its ends. If the central authority in Indonesia continues to weaken, look for an increase in Filipino-style *bossism*—regional bosses moving into the political vacuum with the backing of parapolitical and paramilitary militias. As the violence in Maluku has already illustrated, much of the rivalry among bosses may be given an ethnic or religious color. Look for more of this sort of violence if Wahid is toppled.

Economic Stabilization and the Vulnerable Presidency. The Suharto regime collapsed not just because of its many political abuses but because it could not stem the severe economic recession. Wahid's limited experience as an economic manager and the strong legacy of corruption in the state administration will continue to pose serious challenges to his efforts to give his government legitimacy. If his economic programs fail to take hold, look for elements of the People's Consultative Assembly (MPR) to mount another campaign to remove Wahid in August 2001. (The MPR is legally entitled to evaluate the president's performance each year.) More generally, look for continuing firefights between the president and representatives in the assembly who want to move Indonesia away from a presidential system of government to a more vigorously parliamentary one.

Modernists vs. Traditionalists. Indonesia is politically divided not just between secular and Islamic nationalists, but between modernist and traditionalist Muslim nationalists. In the years to come, look for Amien Rais, the leader of Indonesia's largest modernist Muslim organization (the Muhammadiyah), to position himself for a run for the presidency. Conservatively democratic in his basic vision, Rais is less liberal than Wahid on matters of religious pluralism. He will fail unless he can expand his political base beyond that of the modernist Muslim community. Look to see whether he forges an alliance with the moderate and largely secular nationalist wing of Golkar, the party created by Suharto. If he attempts such a move, we can expect to see an end-run around Rais by hardline elements in the modernist community—perhaps in alliance with segments of the military long hostile to him.

Military Revival? Discredited by its record of human rights abuses and its alliance with Suharto, the military at the moment is the weakest it has been in the entire history of the Indonesian republic. It is down but not out, however. Look for Prabowo Subianto and his allies to attempt to block civilian investigations into human rights abuses. If they succeed, look for Prabowo to attempt to build a new alliance between conservative military officers and hardline Muslims. If Wahid falls from the presidency, the single most important figure standing in the way of such a program will be Amien Rais. But look for pressure from conservatives in the Muhammadiyah to block investigations of rights abuses, and pressure on Rais to forge a reconciliation with military conservatives.

References

Bresnan, John. *Managing Indonesia: Managing the Modern Political Economy*. New York: Columbia University Press, 1993.

Burton, Greg, and Greg Fealy, eds., *Nahdlatul Ulama, Traditional Islam and Modernity in Indonesia*. Clayton, Australia: Monash Asia Institute, 1996.

Eickelman, Dale F. and Jon W. Anderson. *New Media in the Muslim World: The Emerging Public Sphere*. Bloomington: University of Indiana Press, 1999.

Eickelman, Dale F. and James Piscatori. *Muslim Politics*. Princeton: Princeton University Press, 1996.

Esposito, John L., and John O. Voll, *Islam and Democracy*. New York: Oxford University Press, 1996.

Geertz, Clifford. *The Religion of Java*. New York: Free Press, 1960.

Feillard, Andrée. *Islam et Armée dans l'Indonésie Contemporaine*. Paris: L'Harmattan, 1995.

Hall, John A. "In Search of Civil Society," in Hall, ed., *Civil Society: Theory, History, Comparison*. Cambridge, UK: Polity Press, 1995. Pp. 1-31.

Robert W. Hefner. *Civil Islam: Muslims and Democratization in Indonesia*. Princeton: Princeton University Press, 2000.

_____. "Islam and Nation in the Post-Suharto Era," in Adam Schwarz and Jonathan Paris, *The Politics of Post-Suharto Indonesia*. New York: Council of Foreign Relations, 1999. Pp. 40-72.

_____. "Islamization and Democratization in Indonesia," in Hefner and Patricia Horvatich, eds., *Islam in an Era of Nation-States: Politics and Religious Renewal in Muslim Southeast Asia*. Honolulu: University of Hawaii Press, 1997. Pp. 75-127.

_____. "Religion: Evolving Pluralism," in Donald K. Emmerson, ed., *Indonesia Beyond Suharto*. Armonk, NY: M.E. Sharpe, 1999. Pp. 205-36.

Hull, Terence H., and Gavin W. Jones, "Demographic Perspectives," in Hal Hill, ed., *Indonesia's New Order: The Dynamics of Socio-Economic Transformation*. Honolulu: University of Hawaii Press, 1994. Pp. 123-78.

Huntington, Samuel P. *The Clash of Civilizations and the Remaking of World Order*. New York: Simon & Schuster, 1996.

Jones, Gavin W., and Chris Manning, "Labour Force and Employment during the 1980s," in Anne Booth, ed., *The Oil Boom and After: Indonesian Economic Policy and Performance in the Soeharto Era*. Kuala Lumpur: Oxford University Press, 1992. Pp. 363-410.

Juergensmeyer, Mark. *The New Cold War? Religious Nationalism Confronts the Secular State*. Berkeley: University of California Press, 1993.

Kurzman, Charles. *Liberal Islam: A Sourcebook*. New York: Oxford University Press, 1998.

Lindholm, Tore, and Kari Vogt. *Islamic Law Reform and Human Rights: Challenges and Rejoinders*. Copenhagen: Nordic Human Rights Publications, 1993.

Meeker, Michael E. "The New Muslim Intellectuals in the Republic of Turkey," in Richard Tapper, ed., *Islam in Modern Turkey: Religion, Politics, and Literature in a Secular State*. London: I.B. Tauris, 1991. Pp. 189-219.

Mortimer, Rex. *Indonesian Communism under Sukarno: Ideology and Politics, 1959-1965*. Ithaca: Cornell University Press, 1974.

Norton, Augustus Richard. *Civil Society in the Middle* East, Vol. 1. Leiden: E.J. Brill, 1995.

Putnam, Robert D. *Making Democracy Work: Civic Traditions in Modern Italy*. Princeton: Princeton University Press, 1993.

Reid, Anthony. *Southeast Asia in the Age of Commerce, 1450-1680*, Volume Two: *Expansion and Crisis*. New Haven: Yale University Press, 1993

Ricklefs, M.C. *A History of Modern Indonesia Since c. 1300*, Second Edition. Stanford: Stanford University Press, 1993.

Robison, Richard. *Indonesia: The Rise of Capital*. North Sydney, Australia: Allen & Unwin, 1986.

Shirashi, Takashi. "The Indonesian Military in Politics," in Adam Schwarz and Jonathan Paris, *The Politics of Post-Suharto Indonesia*. New York: Council of Foreign Relations, 1999. Pp. 73-86.

Swarz, Adam. *A Nation in Waiting: Indonesia's Search for Stability*. Boulder: Westview, 2000.

van der Veer, Peter. *Religious Nationalism: Hindus and Muslims in India*. Berkeley: University of California Press, 1994.

Woodward, Mark R. *Islam in Java: Normative Piety and Mysticism in the Sultanate of Yogyakarta*. Tucson: University of Arizona Press, 1989.

VI

Religious Freedom and Religious Conflict in Africa

Rosalind I. J. Hackett

The vast continent of Africa, with over fifty countries and more than 2,000 ethnic groups, offers untold religious diversity. And with its ongoing disengagement from colonialist structures and move toward more democratic systems of government, the place of religion presents a significant challenge. The challenge is compounded by Africa's pluralizing and globalizing religious landscape.

It is an oversimplification to characterize Africa as having two major religious traditions—Islam and Christianity—against a background of local forms of indigenous belief and practice. There are not only many Islams and Christianities that have been brought to the continent and taken root there but also the creative and innovative responses of Africans themselves in forming their own religious movements. Sometimes these latter emerged as forms of political resistance—for example, the Antonian movement, whose founder, Dona Béatrice or Kimpa Vita, was burned at the stake in 1706 for her efforts in trying to turn a Portuguese Catholic mission into the Kongo Catholic Church. For other local prophets, the quest was more one of cultural and spiritual relevance. By emphasizing dreams, visions, healing, and spirit possession, they were at once validating their own cultural roots and actively negotiating new indigenous forms of Christianity and, to a lesser extent, Islam. The main thrust of this religious self-determination began during colonialism (from end of 19th to beginning of 20th century) and was most marked in those areas that had been missionized by Protestantism. The impact of these thousands of religious movements and their more transnational successors, the evangelical/Pentecostal/charismatic churches, has been considerable.

In the 1980s, while teaching religious studies at a Nigerian university, I conducted with my students an extensive ethnographic and historical study of religious plurality in the mid-sized southeastern Nigerian town of Calabar, close to the Cameroon border. Since then, I have continued to monitor the remarkable growth of indigenous and exogenous religious groups in many parts of Africa. The ways that Africans themselves grapple with religious changes at both the local, translocal, and transnational levels have both intrinsic interest and comparative value. Of special importance are the ways in which questions of religious difference turn into situations of interreligious tension and conflict. Africa as a whole seems to bear out Pope John Paul II's prediction that the relationship between Christians and Muslims is central to peace and social stability in the new millennium.[1] While religious violence in Africa has not achieved the notoriety it has in other regions of the world,[2] there are nonetheless some highly pertinent examples of it arising from Muslim-Christian tensions—in Nigeria, Sudan, South Africa, Ghana, Mali, and Zambia, to name but a few countries.[3]

Religious tension and conflict are on the rise in postcolonial Africa because the terms of religious co-existence have changed. The failure of the African nation-state to provide for its citizens has created a vacuum frequently filled by religious groups. Thus the national scene becomes more competitive as religious institutions that were formerly privileged by colonial regimes find themselves as just one of the players in a new pluralistic dispensation. Meanwhile, the incursions of the global market economy render some religious options more attractive than others—especially those that place a high value on prosperity and upward mobility. Some religious groups may even offer the means to this end in the form of networking, educational scholarships, employment, literacy, or skills training. In addition, human rights discourse increasingly pervades civil society and national politics. It is not uncommon now to hear African people claiming their constitutional rights to freedom of expression and freedom of religion—often in the media and in educational institutions.

The religious dimensions of African life are complex. Compared to the kind of religion most Americans are familiar with, religion in Africa is less individualistic and more group-related; more materially grounded, and more intimately connected to relations of power, whether beneficent or maleficent. Concepts of power are less differentiated than in Western thinking. For example, there is a vast scholarly literature on African politicians' manipulation of religious symbols, agents, and rituals to serve their own ends. The Cameroon economist Celestin Monga has noted the many African heads of state who have sought photo opportunities with the pope in the course of his visits to the African continent. He also has expressed his considerable skepticism about religious elites exercising any critical, prophetic role because of their readiness to be co-opted by the state (Monga 1996). This process has occurred in the new South Africa, where many of the nation's anti-apartheid activists who also were leading religious figures have now assumed government positions.

It has become fashionable to see religion as implicated in the waves of identity politics around the world. Yet it is equally if not more important to

---

[1] Muslim-Christian relations were the subject of the BBC World Service program, "Talking Point" on January 3, 2000.

[2] University of California at Santa Barbara professor Mark Juergensmeyer informed me that, apart from Egypt, Africa did not feature in his recent book, *Terror in the Mind of God*, because "Africans did not plant bombs."

[3] These feature in the more sensationalist account of Christian persecution around the world by Paul Marshall, *Their Blood Cries Out* .

understand how religion is linked to *survival* in the lives of many Africans. Indeed, this existential dimension of religion is all too often neglected in favor of political interpretations of the role of religion in contemporary Africa. Whether they are battling disease or poverty, or enduring political misrule, Africans turn to religious strategies for interpreting and coping with life's contingencies in ways that the average Westerner would not comprehend. It is likewise important to note that at the level of everyday life, religious ideas may act as sources of "spiritual insecurity." A prime example is the persistence of witchcraft beliefs and practices even in the most "advanced" sectors of African society. Stories of occult influences and happenings that circulate as rumors or in the popular press seem to subvert the certainties of modern life. For example, Madumo, the subject of Adam Ashforth's recent book on witchcraft in Soweto, attributes the rise in witchcraft accusations to the high unemployment in South Africa. Overall, there now exists an excellent body of scholarship on the phenomenon of witchcraft accusations.[4]

The manifold historical factors that have shaped current religion-and-state relationships throughout Africa need to be underlined—because these have has often been overlooked in press coverage of African affairs. One could cite the late Zairean dictator Mobutu Seke Seko's manipulation of religious leaders to serve his own political ends in former Zaire; the religious justification for the apartheid system in South Africa; the privileging of Islam in northern Nigeria by the British colonial authorities; President Jerry Rawlings' ideological battles with the churches in Ghana and his politicized support for Islam; and the missionary education of great African leaders such as Julius Nyerere and Nelson Mandela. Tempting as it may be to revisit some of these cases, however, let us consider two more recent and interrelated phenomena that are currently heightening religious tensions in various parts of Africa—namely, the resurgence of radical religious revivalism, and the growth of the mass media.

My purpose here is not to heighten negative perceptions of Africa, which are rampant enough already, but rather to bring Africa's religious flash points and conflict-resolution strategies into the conversation about religious pluralism and freedom around the globe. The increasing prominence of concerns about religious persecution and conflict is due in no small part to the signing into U.S. law in October 1998 of the International Religious Freedom Act, and its mandated annual State Department report on International Religious Freedom (published in September). It can also be traced to greater awareness of the renewed roles of religion in the public sphere. Of course many Africans would say that religion has never *not* had a strong public dimension in the African context. Even the most secularist efforts at state creation have co-opted religious leaders and drawn on religio-cultural discourse to legitimate state

---

[4] In 1998, the *African Studies Review* dedicated an entire issue to the subject.

power. Mainline or historic church leaders have played key roles in the democ-ratization processes in many African countries in the last decade or so. The report card on the churches' influence, however, is mixed. For example, in his recent book on the public role of African Christianity, University of London professor Paul Gifford sees signs of hope in Ghana and Uganda, but growing despair in Cameroon and corruption and uncaring attitudes in the Christian nation of Zambia.

Perhaps the greatest social, and in some cases political, impact has rather come from the corner of the Muslim and Christian revivalists who have been growing in influence in various parts of Africa since the 1970s. They attract in particular the youth. They vary in their degrees of radicalism and militancy. The targets of their reform may be fellow Muslims (e.g., anti-Sufi against Sufi) and Christians ("born-again" or "spirit-filled" against "dead" Christians) or indeed people of other traditions. Elements of religious fundamentalism may be identified among both Christians and Muslims but it does not suffice to describe the movements themselves as such. In West Africa notably, the influ-ence of the Christian evangelical/pentecostal/charismatic movements is felt across the Christian spectrum. Their ideas and materials circulate readily, aided by market flows, and by the loose yet interconnected structures of the movements and their key players. While some African political leaders have publicly or privately identified themselves with these conservative religious forces, others perceive them as subversive and/or retrogressive. It would be wrong to suggest that the spread of Christian (and Muslim) revivalism is a pre-dominantly militant form of religious movement. But I am arguing that their ready recourse to militant discourse and practices (i.e., use of language such as "crusades," "God's army," "jihad," etc.) has noticeably heightened tensions and accentuated differences between religious groups. Their proselytizing prac-tices have transgressed time-honored boundaries and subverted traditional forms of authority. Such groups generally owe no allegiances to an historic, central authority; they are self-motivated and self-structured, drawing on glob-alizing repertoires of belief and practice. In the case of Christian revivalism, it is argued by Gifford and others that such movements are ideologically domi-nated by (North American) right-wing Christianity, and, as such, are inimical to more radical forces of social development and political reform.[5] There is some truth to this, but it overlooks the role of Africans themselves in actively appropriating and transforming these forms of religious discourse and organi-zation (through personal contact, education/training, literature, mission work, etc.). It also underestimates the transnational, multilateral character of Pentecostal/charismatic Christianity. In 1994 I received a grant to track

---

[5] See the summary of right-wing Christian Groups active in South Africa, Namibia, and Zimbabwe compiled by the *Review of African Political Economy* from a paper presented by Harald Winkler to the Catholic Institute for International Relations (CIIR) Conference on Faith and Development, October 1989 .

African evangelists in Asia. I visited Singapore, Malaysia, the Philippines, and South Korea to document and analyze this growing South-South religious connections between African Pentecostal organizations and their Asian counterparts. The growing influence of Pentecostal churches of Brazilian origin from the 1990s, such as the Universal Church of the Kingdom of God, also merits attention. I have visited their branches in Nairobi and Durban. In Kenya they made heavy use of the media, attracting many people as well as criticism for their strong emphasis on healing and immediate relief from suffering and poverty, set within a theology of victimization. I was told that the Brazilian leaders had now moved to South Africa.

As part of their expansionist orientation, it is the Christian revivalist groups in particular that have realized the potential of the growing mass media industry in Africa. Whether by purchasing air-time on economically strapped government radio and television stations, taking advantage of new outlets in the private media sector, or linking up with international television networks, these newer religious organizations have developed an influence beyond their demographic base of support. Ghana is a case in point. While it is not legally permissible to run a religious broadcasting station, Ghana's charismatic organizations have flooded the airwaves of the new FM stations with their gospel music, their ideas (via call-in programs), and even their pastors as announcers.[6] The producers say that this is what people want. Frequently the audience is young—men and women between the ages of 20 and 40 who are drawn to the educated, wealthy, and "new-look" pastors. The pastors' lifestyles are trendy and their services upbeat. In the words of Martin Lwanga, the station manager Power FM, a Christian radio station that broadcasts from Kampala, Uganda, "It is a new culture. You have an old culture that has not changed since the 1930s....This is an answer to that. The old order is dying."[7]

In fact, it is more than ever possible to argue that the media in Africa constitute the new venue for interreligious encounter and religious self-representation. Muslims have generally been slower on the uptake to avail themselves of modern media technologies, because of widely held beliefs that the media are Christian-dominated. Some more progressive Muslim groups, notably in southwestern Nigeria, have been seeking to persuade wealthy Muslims in the local communities to fund greater coverage of Islam in the broadcast media. The issue of representation is both sensitive and crucial. In Cameroon, where broadcasting is government-controlled, the Muslim community has always been granted proportional public space. This has arguably led to more harmonious relations.

For Muslims in South Africa the situation is different. While they have

---

6   JOY FM, the first of the Ghanaian FM stations, even bills itself as "the station that brings you closer to heaven." Peace FM makes an even bolder claim: "This is the station that praises the Lord Almighty like no other."

7   The Nairobi *East African*, June 2, 2000.

gained access to the media and have been able to air some of their own programs on the radio in particular, there is evidence that they are still subject to
distorted and prejudiced representations. These were the findings of a Muslim
media group, the Media Review Network, which reported to the South African
Human Rights Commission in Johannesburg in early March of 2000.[8] The
report described the South African media as generating "Islamophobia"
through a demonizing and stereotyping of Islam, notably in connection with a
series of bombings in Cape Town and East Africa. According to the report, the
media readily identified the religion of perpetrators of violence if Muslims
were involved, but "deliberately omit the religious affiliation when non-
Muslims are involved."

The Truth and Reconciliation Commission, whose proceedings dominated the South African media for months on end, is another bone of contention.
At the Parliament of the World's Religions in Cape Town in December of
1999, radical Muslim thinkers such as Farid Esack and Rashied Omar spoke
openly of the Commission's Christian bias and failure to mete out justice to the
perpetrators of the apartheid regime. They also discussed the preference
among many Muslims for reparation over reconciliation.

In Ghana, something of the converse occurred when President Jerry
Rawlings allotted exceptional blocks of television airtime to Louis Farrakhan
when the latter visited Ghana on different occasions. Many Christians felt
that the President was courting Ghana's Muslim minority (around 30 percent
of the population) for political purposes. The exploitation of this national
medium was a most powerful and controversial act. It seems that, given the
unpopularity and unconstitutionality of controlling and (potentially) restrict-
ing the activities of purportedly subversive religious groups through registration mechanisms, some governments see media censorship as a more acceptable tool for co-opting or excluding religious ideologies. In many instances, it
is only mainline and/or officially sanctioned religious groups that are invited
to broadcast and at strictly controlled times. Frequently, broadcasters have to
respect format and content guidelines. Such restrictions are inevitably alien-
ating and frustrating even as they seek to minimize religious difference and
enhance nationalist sentiments. But with the growing commercialization of
the media throughout Africa, and also the explosion of small-scale media
technology and production (audio and video), they are increasingly difficult to
enforce. Often it comes down to self-censorship on the part of the various
religious constituencies.

Finally, the political economy of the African mass media is being transformed. Financially strapped government television stations find it hard to
resist the slickly presented videotapes of American evangelists—often provid-

---

[8] Although I was informed that this was a small group by no means representative of the Muslim
     community as a whole.

ed *gratis* and sometimes with financial inducements. This is evident, for example, in the Democratic Republic of Congo, where daytime programming of American televangelists in a town outside Kinshasa was over 50 percent, and in Ghana, where the Christian Broadcasting Network (CBN) started regular programs on the conservative Ghana Broadcasting Company's television station at the beginning of the year. Back in the 1980s, the Nigerian Television Authority was even airing Pat Robertson's CBN news at prime time! Trinity Broadcasting Network (TBN), which enjoyed special relations with the Ciskei homeland government in the 1980s, established the first independent religious station in Africa and is currently developing a South African network.

On a visit in the summer of 1999, I picked up on the excitement over the launching of Kenya's first commercial Christian television network, Family TV, and its radio affiliate, Family FM. The Dutch managing director was unabashedly promoting a model of American religiosity and musical performance. For many younger Kenyans the appeal of the gospel funk is obvious; more ambivalence could be heard among older churchgoers, who perceived its potential for homogenizing their religious tradition into standard-brand American evangelicalism. The South African Broadcasting Commission is holding out against such attractions in the interest of religious and cultural diversity, despite having had its funding for religious programming cut in half over a year ago.

It is not only internal questions of programming and sponsorship that determine power relations among religious organizations, but also external factors. During the recent outbreak of religious violence in Nigeria, one local reporter lashed out at the BBC World Service for privileging Muslims by having a Hausa language service (the language of the North of the country which is Muslim-dominated). He argued that this was helping fuel the tensions in the country. So while the BBC were unlikely to have incited violence, and the Nigerian media were in fact praised for exhibiting restraint during the riots by President Olusegun Obasanjo, the symbolic significance of an external power, and the former colonial power at that, seemingly perpetuating their pro-Muslim sympathies, should not be underestimated.

Of course, the actual reporting of incidents of religious conflict is critical to managing and manipulating them. The public media provide a forum (for example, via press statements and rejoinders, and letters to the editor) for airing fears and tensions between religious groups and for setting the record straight. But more often than not, because of their vested interests and concern for sales, they become an extension of local religious tensions, often escalating them to national levels. This is well illustrated in the recent and ongoing "To Drum or Not to Drum" controversy in Ghana.

In the coastal part of Accra—traditionally the home of the Gan people who make up 10 to15 percent of the population of the Greater Accra Region—there is a traditional ban on drumming as a prelude to the annual Homowo festival period. Some Pentecostalists refused to accept the taboo and serious clashes have resulted over the last couple of years. Questions of territorial integrity and freedom of worship have been strongly articulated on both sides. The Commissioner for Human Rights and Administrative Justice, Emile Short, condemned the ban as unconstitutional, while the Accra Metropolitan Authority came out in favor of it. Some observers reported to me that they felt that the whole incident had been unnecessarily polarized, sensationalized, and politicized by the media.[9] But there was little doubt that the whole affair sparked a national debate about uncontrolled religious growth, noise pollution, freedom of worship, and the relevance of cultural traditions to modern life. In the end, ecumenical responses prevented any recurrence of the altercations that took place in May 1999. A national association of charismatic and Christian churches, operating as a kind of task force within the Ghana Pentecostal Council, was inaugurated in late 1999 to address the issues. Then, in April of 2000, a forum of religious bodies that included Muslims, Christians, and traditionalists, issued a joint declaration and recommended the formation of a Standing Committee "to monitor and manage any misunderstandings arising out of the celebration or observance of customs, traditions, festivals and worship in the Greater Accra Region."[10] This and the cooperation by several churches was reported positively as a "search for peace" by the government-linked news organs, the *Daily Graphic* and the *Ghanaian Times*—although, by contrast, an independent newspaper reported how youth from both sides were gearing up to enforce or resist the ban on drumming and noise-making.[11]

A less happy example of the interaction of religion and media is the recent burning of Islamic writings by a Christian evangelical pastor on Kongo television. Street riots resulted from this act of religious violence committed live as public spectacle.

In Nigeria itself, the Cross incident, as it came to be known, epitomizes how a local religious dispute can spin out of control through media exposure. When the new mosque at the University of Ibadan was completed in 1985-86, Muslims objected to seeing the Protestant chapel when they were at prayers. The ensuing wrangling over territory, screens, and the taking down of sacred symbols led to angry confrontations up to the national level. In this case, according to Rev. Father Dr. Matthew Hassan Kukah, an astute and experienced commentator on Nigeria's religious and political scene, "[t]he media has helped in fanning and sustaining the embers of bigotry."

It should not be underestimated just how much the eyes of Africa are

---

[9] A leading example of this is the widely-read Christian newspaper, *The Watchman*, edited by Pastor Divine Kumah, which focuses a great deal of attention on what it sees as Muslim threats to Christian interests in Ghana and the persecution of Christians worldwide.

[10] I am grateful to Rev. Dr. Sam S. Quarcoopome and Benedict Assorow for supplying this information.

[11] *Dispatch*, April 19-25, 2000.

directed toward Nigeria and its ups and downs. Black Africa's most populous country is viewed as a type of lodestar. When the potential fragmentation of Nigeria is talked about—as it has been in connection with the recent attempt by some northern states to impose Muslim traditional law (*shari`a*) as the principal legal code and the resultant outbreak of religious violence—there is a sense of alarm among other African countries. For it is felt that if Nigeria, with its material wealth, cannot manage and meet the needs of its peoples, woe to Africa's less wealthy and powerful countries. Nigeria also raises the specter of religious polarization that, in many Nigerians' minds, is epitomized by Sudan. (It is interesting to note that Nigeria's new president Obasanjo served as a mediator in Sudan in the late 1980s and early 1990s.)

Nigeria was once proud of its record of religious tolerance. This record was dealt a severe blow in the late 1970s when Maitatsine, a radical Islamic sect, clashed with political and religious authorities in the northern city of Kano and hundreds of lives were lost.[12] The late 1980s saw a series of riots, again in the north of the country, involving both Muslims and Christians. The considerable loss of life and property, and the way in which the violence spread to other cities, generated concern nationwide. The 1987 Kaduna riots occasioned commissions of inquiry and considerable press coverage.

Sporadic incidents through the 1990s kept alive fears of religion either as a dominant cause of civil instability or as a contributory factor in ethnic or political conflict. But it was in 1999, following efforts to include a provision for *shari`a* in the new national constitution, that feelings started to run high again over Muslim moves toward greater self-determination and revived Christian fears of the Islamization of Nigeria. In April of that year Dr. Sunday Mbang, the vocal President of the influential Christian Association of Nigeria (an organization formed to defend Christian interests), declared that the association was ready for a religious conflict that potentially could be "worse than that of Lebanon."

The situation became explosive in late 1999 when five northern Nigerian states went ahead and introduced *shari`a*. The most serious loss of life and destruction of property occurred in the strategic city of Kaduna when Christians demonstrated in April and May of 2000 against the likely introduction of *shari`a* there. Nigerians were shocked at the cycles of attack and revenge that were unleashed in the north and then spread to the southeast and southwest of the country. Three of the northern states then bowed to pressure and claimed they would revert to their earlier, more limited application of *shari`a*. But in June another state, Kano, announced a full implementation *shari`a* (pending the training of judges and other personnel). The situation remained volatile, with non-Muslims fearing harassment despite the Emir of

---

[12] There is an abundant popular and academic literature on Nigeria's interreligious problems (see Kukah 1993, Kukah 1996, Falola 1998, Williams 1995, and Ilesanmi, 1997).

Kano's broadcast assurance that the launching of *shari`a* should be considered by every Muslim as "the commencement of peace, tolerance and love between Moslems as well as with their neighbors 'because it is prescribed by Islam.'" Journalists of national dailies in Kaduna issued a press release in June through the local chapter of the Nigerian Union of Journalists condemning attacks on their personal security by those bent on silencing their critical reporting on the *shari`a* issue.

A noteworthy aspect of this religious conflict is the increased involvement of youths through their respective revivalist organizations. More militant than their elders, young people tend to be the first line of attack or defense when tensions arise—thanks in some measure to Nigeria's high unemployment rate, which has created cadres of frustrated youth always ready to swing into action. Reports of the greater availability of arms around the country has only raised the stakes. Nor should the heightened involvement of Saudi Arabia in African affairs be overlooked. Specifically, the Saudis have been training Nigerian Muslims in connection with the implementation of *shari`a*.

As usual, Nigerians themselves wasted no time in analyzing these very troubling developments and proffering a variety of interpretations, entirely in keeping with the complex nature of civil unrest in the country. There was a general consensus that the unrest was religious, albit rife with political significance and manipulation. To be sure, a few individuals, such as the well-known Catholic Bishop Olorunfemi Onaiyekan, sought to deny this instead placing blame on persons intent on destroying democratic processes and destabilizing the Obasanjo government. But this explanation should be understood as a religious leader seeking to portray "true" religion (Christian or Muslim) as purely good and peaceable.

President Obasanjo, a Baptist and a retired military general, for months refrained from making any public statements on the crisis. Speaking at a Pentecostal conference in December of 1999, he revealed that he had become a pastor while in prison and advocated prayer as a means of resolving the crises in Nigeria. As the situation worsened, his language became more forceful. In his March 1 address to the nation he talked about the "carnage and devastation" that he witnessed in Kaduna, and his disbelief that "Nigerians were capable of such barbarism against each other."

It is important and interesting to note how this particular *shari`a* controversy and the ensuing religious riots rapidly became an issue in other parts of Africa. On March 1, for example, Zambian Christian and Religious Affairs Deputy Minister Peter Chintala welcomed the suspension of Islamic *shari`a* law by the three Nigerian states as a "righteous move in line with God's desire for love and peace in the world." The minister reminded Zambians that although Zambia was constitutionally a Christian nation, it was tolerant of other religions. Yet he also challenged Christians to pray hard and ensure that the Bible prevailed over other religious beliefs.[13]

It is important to recognize that such events are not only picked up by local and international news agencies around Africa but also recirculated via the Internet. Academics are not insignificant players here as are Africans living overseas. Increasing numbers of Africans living in "diasporic" communities debate passionately their national and cultural interests via Naija-Net or Cameroon-Net, etc. As these discussions filter back and forth, scholars have only begun to consider how they may be influencing local debates. Given the posturing and "flaming" that occur in this intriguingly intimate and yet impersonal communicative medium, fervent opinions and conspiracy theories abound. Yet even as it expands the scope of tension and confrontation, such use of the Internet (which can only increase exponentially) points to the greater sense of interconnectedness and interdependency in today's world. Altogether, the new information technologies are challenging familiar cultural categories and helping to redefine communities. They deserve far more attention from observers in the media as well as the academy.

The area of conflict resolution in Africa merits some discussion, because of the range of methods that Africans are deploying to combat religious conflict, and because the efforts being undertaken to promote and protect religious freedom need to be evaluated. The latter are sometimes multilateral, involving international as well as local bodies. Both the Roman Catholic Church and the Lutheran church have a longstanding interest in interreligious dialogue and conflict resolution. Yet Africans also commonly look to their indigenous traditions and traditional leaders as a resource for tolerance and peace. In Cameroon, for example, a non-governmental organization known as the Ecumenical Service for Peace has been working with traditional priests and drawing on local religious resources (leaders, values) to help solve ethnic conflict in Cameroon. Workshops on conflict resolution are organized by CODESRIA—a social science think tank for African scholars based in Dakar, Senegal.

Similarly, there exists a large body of literature on—and much discussion of—religious tolerance in Nigeria at both the popular and official levels. The decline of religious tolerance is a matter of serious concern to the majority of Nigerians and is preached about and pronounced upon on many occasions. High-level bodies such as the Nigerian Inter-Religious Council (NIREC) are charged with, in the words of the President, "the responsibility of promoting ideals of peaceful coexistence, especially among the various religions in our country." More grassroots initiatives play their part too. I was particularly impressed by a very humble, yet clearly effective, organization, the Muslim-Christian Youth Dialogue Forum, founded by a local Muslim and a Christian

---

[13] The *Times of Zambia*, March 2, 2000.

evangelist to combat ignorance and intolerance among the youth in Kaduna. The Muslim had lost relatives in a riot, and the evangelist had lost part of his own arm. The two somehow came together and decided that it was better to make peace and not war. Training and financial assistance are now gradually being offered by a variety of sources to support their work.

As an educator, I have been keen to see programs in the schools and universities to combat religious intolerance.[14] These now exist in Kenya, Nigeria, Ghana, Zimbabwe, Malawi, and South Africa. But my research and experience reveals a contrary trend of religious conservatism and identity politics gaining ground in many educational institutions. This can be attributed to the expansion of revivalist religious groups and to greater parental and community involvement/interference in the education system to ensure their religious rights. For example, I have heard it frequently said by Christian parents that they do not want their children learning about Islam in school. But it is vital to distinguish between teaching religion and teaching *about* religion. Nor can education about religious diversity be excluded from the curriculum in African schools. For educational institutions can easily become micro-battlegrounds in larger religious wars.

As I have suggested above, everyone is agreed upon the central importance of the news media, both local and international, in situations of religious conflict. Indeed, Jeremy Gunn, the former Director of Research of the U.S. Commission on International Religious Freedom, even goes as far as to call the media the key factor in determining responses of tolerance or intolerance.[15]

It is undeniably a challenge to evaluate the role of religion in situations of conflict in Africa. There is the temptation to under- or overrate its importance, especially when considering questions of ethnicity or nationalism, since they are all so closely connected in the African context. Why does religious conflict arise in some African countries and not in others? Degrees of repression, types of leadership, economic conditions, levels of literacy, the history and current nature of missionary activity, demographic balance, reliability of the security forces, and colonialist hangovers—all must be taken into account.

A major reason for the volatility of Nigeria is the even balance of Muslims and Christians (exact figures are not known since religious affiliation was expressly left out of the last census in 1991 for fears that the results could be divisive and/or manipulated). This results in greater competition over the national pie. But Nigeria is hardly an exception. With the globalization of communications, economic forces, and cultural flows, and with what John

---

[14]   On June 15, 2000, information circulated on the Internet about a religious group in Ghana that combines both Islam and Christianity in a quest for peace. Called "Zetaheal" (Hebrew for "Lean on me for your salvation"), it was founded by a dressmaker named Comfort Narh. In the article by Kwaku Sakyi-Addo for BBC News Online, "Christians and Muslims in Harmony," the members are shown dressed in white and worshipping together.

[15]   Personal communication, Boston, November 22, 1999.

Thompson calls the "mediaization" of society, issues of religious identity, representation, and rights, are gaining prominence in many parts of the world. In Africa, longstanding traditions of religious tolerance are being sorely tested by a potent mix of religious revivalism, media expansion, and Christian and Muslim rivalry.

Issues to Keep an Eye on

HIV/AIDS. The United Nations estimates that of the 34 million people affected by HIV/AIDS worldwide, 24 million are in Africa. Some 2.2 million Africans died of AIDS in 1999. Life expectancy in most affected areas has declined by almost 20 percent and more than half of those contracting HIV/AIDS are young people between the ages of 16 and 24. As awareness and anger increase regarding this epidemic, we are seeing and will see a growing involvement of religious organizations in managing the crisis. This is long overdue, given the key role played by many of Africa's churches in the health-care sector. The perception by many that the disease is linked to supernatural forces, e.g. witchcraft, is undoubtedly behind the inaction of many mainstream religious organizations and accounts for efforts by many traditional healers to counteract the "slimming disease." Quite frequently, these cultural questions get lost behind the statistics and medical evidence.

Freedom of Religion and the Challenge of Religious Pluralism. Religious pluralism and its management assume a growing importance in African social and political discourse—one that is generally framed in terms of fears that the proliferation of religious groups constitute a threat to national integration and a recipe for economic and social exploitation. Actions taken range from reducing the influence of religious formations in the public sphere (as in former Zaire) to a re-mapping of the country along religious lines (as in Nigeria). Registration is generally the mechanism employed by the state to censor or at least limit the activities of disfavored groups. As one might expect, the apparent massacre of close to 800 people in connection with an independent Catholic movement in Uganda known as the Movement for the Restoration of the Ten Commandments of God in March of 2000 caused several African governments (Togo, Kenya, Rwanda, Burundi, Congo and Uganda itself) to clamp down on the activities of "sects" and "cults." These responses need to be seen against the background of development issues, democratization, and new claims to religious freedom, as well as similar actions currently being taken by former colonial powers, such as France, Germany and Belgium.

Impact of Africa's Expanding Media Sector. The commercialization and privatization of the media occasioned by democratization and economic developments has started to reshape the power relations of Africa's religious landscape. Previously mandated religious tolerance and civility on government-owned radio and television is now overridden by the market-driven religious enthusiasm of (mainly) Christian and Muslim revivalists. This causes resentment and tension, and shows every sign of growing in intensity in many locations. The obvious potential of the modern mass media to serve as the principal interface between competing religious groups and as the principal site of the rapid growth of religious revivalism and fundamentalism in many parts of Africa will certainly become more apparent. It will be interesting to observe how much media style and content will be influenced by U.S. and Middle Eastern religious communities, and to what extent Africa serves as a satellite for the empire-building of foreign evangelists.

Youth. Young people represent the crucial social sector to watch for religious trends and developments in Africa. Attracted to the use of modern media and livelier forms of worship, they implicitly or openly provide an important cultural challenge to traditional religious authorities. Empowered and mobilized by revivalist and fundamentalist messages with global connections, they demand the reform of religious and political leaders in the face of moral dislocation, political instability and corruption, and failed economic promises. They are frequently at the forefront of religious conflict and unrest. The devastating effect of HIV/AIDS on Africa's youth, as they find themselves without parents and leaders, and with limited life expectancy, has hardly begun to be appreciated and understood. As an important dimension of civil society, will religious organizations (and if so, which ones) be able to resolve these almost unimagined social problems or will they retreat onto moral high ground?

References

1991a. Evangelical Broadcasting. *Review of African Political Economy* 52:87-88.

1991b. Right-Wing Christian Groups. *Review of African Political Economy* 52:88-93.

An-Na'im, Abdullahi A. and Francis M. Deng, ed. 1990. *Human Rights in Africa: Cross-Cultural Perspectives*. Washington DC: The Brookings Institution.

Ashforth, Adam. 1998. Reflections on Spiritual Insecurity in a Modern African City (Soweto). *African Studies Review* 41 (3):39-68.

_____. 2000. *Madumo: A Man Bewitched*. Chicago: University of Chicago.

Assefa, H., and G. Wachira, eds. 1996. *Peacemaking and Democratisation in Africa:Theoretical Perspectives and Church Initiatives*. Nairobi: East African Educational Publishers.

Banjo, Ayo. 1997. *In the Saddle: A Vice-Chancellor's Story*. Ibadan: Spectrum.

Bastian, Misty. 1993. "Bloodhounds Who Have No Friends": Witchcraft and Locality in the Nigerian Popular Press. In *Modernity and its Malcontents: Ritual and Power in Postcolonial Africa*, edited by J. Comaroff and J. Comaroff. Chicago: University of Chicago.

_____. 1998. Fires, Tricksters and Poisoned Medicines: Popular Cultures of Rumor in Onitsha, Nigeria and Its Markets. *Etnofoor* 11 (2):111-132.

_____. 1999. Nationalism in a Virtual Space: Immigrant Nigerians on the Internet. *West Africa Review* 1 (1).

Bayart, Jean-Francois. 1993. *The State in Africa: the Politics of the Belly*. New York: Longman.

Bongmba, Elias. 1998. Toward a Hermeneutic of Wimbun *Tfu*. *African Studies Review* 41 (3):165-192.

Bourgault, Louise. 1995. *Media in Sub-Saharan Africa*. Philadelphia: University of Pennsylvania Press.

Ciekawy, Diane, and Peter Geschiere. 1998. Containing Witchcraft: Conflicting Scenarios in Postcolonial Africa. *African Studies Review* 41 (3):1-14.

Cochrane, James, John de Gruchy, and Stephen Martin, eds. 1999. *Facing the Truth: South African Faith Communities and the Truth and Reconciliation Commission*. Cape Town, Athens, OH: David Philip/Ohio University Press.

Comaroff, Jean, and John Comaroff, eds. 1993. *Mondernity and Its Malcontents: Ritual and Power in Postcolonial Africa*. Chicago: University of Chicago.

Cox, Harvey. 1996. *Fire from: the Rise of Pentecostal Spirituality and the Reshaping of Religion in the Twenty-first Century*. London: Cassell.

Danmole, H. O. 1999. Media Use of Muslims in South-western Nigeria: Parallels and Comparisons. Paper read at Religion and Media in Africa, at SOAS, London.

Dlamini, Charles. 1994. Culture, Education and Religion. In *Rights and Constitutionalism: the New South African Legal Order*, edited by D. v. Wyk, J. Dugard, d. B. Villiers and D. Davis. Kenwyn, South Africa: Juta & Co.

Falola, Toyin. 1998. *Violence in Nigeria: The Crisis of Religious Politics and Secular Ideologies*. Rochester, NY: University of Rochester Press.

Freston, Paul. 1995. Pentecostalism in Brazil: A Brief History. *Religion* 25:119-134.

Geschiere, Peter. 1997. *The Modernity of Witchcraft: Politics and the Occult in Postcolonial Africa*. Charlottesville: University Press of Virginia.

_____. 1998. Globalization and the Power of Indeterminate Meaning: Witchcraft and Spirit Cults in Africa and East Asia. In *Globalization and Identity*, edited by P. Geschiere and B. Meyer. Oxford: Blackwell.

Gifford, Paul. 1990. Prosperity: A New and Foreign Element in African Christianity. *Religion* 20 (4):373-88.

_____. 1991a. Christian Fundamentalism and Development. *Review of African Political Economy* 52:9-20.

_____. 1991b. *The New Crusaders: Christianity and the New Right in Southern Africa*. London: Pluto.

_____. ed. 1995. *The Christian Churches and the Democratisation of Africa*. Leiden: E. J. Brill.

_____. 1998a. *African Christianity. Its Public Role*. Bloomington, IN: Indiana University Press.

_____. 1998b. Chiluba's Christian Nation: Christianity as a Factor in Zambian Politics 1991-1996. *Journal of Contemporary Religion* 13 (3):363-3871.

Hackett, Rosalind I. J. 1989. *Religion in Calabar: the Religious Life and History of a Nigerian Town*. The Hague and New York: Mouton de Gruyter.

_____. 1996. New Directions and Connections for African and Asian Charismatics. *Pneuma* 18 (1):69-77.

_____. 1998. Charismatic/Pentecostal Appropriation of Media Technologies in Nigeria and Ghana. *Journal of Religion in Africa* 26 (4):1-19.

_____. 1999. Conflict in the Classroom: Educational Institutions as Sites of Religious Tolerance/Intolerance in Nigeria. *Brigham Young University Law Review*.

_____. 1999b. Managing or Manipulating Religious Conflict in the Nigerian Media. Paper read at Edinburgh International Conference on Media, Religion and Culture, at Edinburgh.

_____. 1999c. Radical Christian Revivalism in Nigeria and Ghana: Recent Patterns of Conflict and Intolerance. In *Proselytization and Communal Self-Determination in Africa*, edited by A. A. An-Na'im. Maryknoll, NY: Orbis.

Hastings, Adrian. 1994. *The Church in Africa 1450-1950*. Oxford: Clarendon.

Haynes, Jeff. 1996. *Religion and Politics in Africa*. London: Zed.

Ilesanmi, Simeon O. 1997. *Religious Pluralism and the Nigerian State*. Athens, OH: Ohio University Press.

Kassimir, Ronald. 1998. The Social Power of Religious Organizations and Civil Society: The Catholic Church in Uganda. In *Civil Society and Democracy in Africa: Critical Perspectives*, edited by N. Kasfir. London/Portland, OR: Frank Cass.

Kukah, Matthew Hassan. 1993. *Religion, Politics and Power in Northern Nigeria*. Ibadan: Spectrum.

Kukah, Matthew Hassan and Toyin Falola. 1996. *Religious Militancy and Self-Assertion: Islam and Politics in Nigeria*. Aldershot, U.K.: Avebury.

Larkin, Brian. 1997. Hausa Dramas and the Rise of Video Culture in Nigera. In *Nigerian Video Films*, edited by J. Haynes. Jos: Nigerian Film Corporation

Marishane, Jeffrey. 1991. Prayer, Profit and Power: US Religious Right and Foreign Policy. *Review of African Political Economy* 52:73-117.

Marshall, Paul. 1997. *Their Blood Cries Out*. Dallas: Word Publishing.

Marshall, Ruth. 1991. Power in the Name of Jesus. *Review of African Political Economy* 52:21-37.

_____. 1995. "God is Not a Democrat: Pentecostalism and Democratisation in Nigeria." In *The Christan Churches and the Democratisation of Africa*, edited by P. Gifford. Leiden: E. J. Brill.

Monga, Celestin. 1996. *The Anthropology of Anger: Civil Society and Democracy in Africa*. Boulder, CO: Lynne Rienner.

Peel, J. D. Y. 1968. *Aladura: a Religious Movement among the Yoruba*. London: International African Institute.

Poewe, Karla, ed. 1994. *Charismatic Christianity as Global Culture*. Columbia, SC: University of South Carolina.

Ranger, Terence O. 1986. Religious Movements and Politics in Sub-Saharan Africa. *African Studies Review* 29 (2):1-69.

Roberts, Pepe, and David Seddon. 1991. Fundamentalism in Africa: Religion and Politics. *Review of African Political Economy* 52:3-8.

Rudolph, Susanne Hoeber and James Piscatori, ed. 1997. *Transnational Religion and Fading States*. Boulder: Westview Press.

Sabar-Friedman, Galia. 1997. Church and State in Kenya 1986-92: the Churches' Involvement in the 'Game of Change'. *African Affairs* 96:25-52.

Sanneh, Lamin. 1997. *The Crown and the Turban: Muslims and West African Pluralism*. Boulder, CO: Westview Press.

Stensvold, Anne. 1999. A Wave of Conversion: Protestantism in Cape Verde. *Religion* 29 (4):337-346.

Thornton, John K. 1998. *The Kongolese Saint Anthony : Dona Beatrix Kimpa Vita and the Antonian Movement*. New York: Cambridge University Press.

VII

The News About Religion in Latin America

Daniel H. Levine

The cliché has it that a picture is worth a thousand words. So let's begin
with a picture, and see where it takes us. I took the photo on this page in
1968, in the Guatemalan market town of Solalá. I remember the scene vividly;
only much later did I grasp its meaning. The photograph shows a Protestant
preacher working a crowd in the market. The majority of Guatemalans are
Indians, the audience is clearly made up of Indian men and women, and the
speaker, I remember, was preaching the gospel in Kakchiquel, the language of
the region. Holding a Bible in his hands, he illustrated his sermon by pointing
to a hand-painted canvas that depicted Heaven, Hell, the temptations of this
world, and the ways of the righteous and of the sinner. The canvas made me
think of *Pilgrim's Progress*. I found the scene stirring enough to save the slide

for more than three decades, but at the time it seemed little more than an interesting sideshow. The preacher, and indeed the whole scene, did not fit into any accepted scheme of things. In retrospect, it is easy to see this preacher as a precursor of the wave of Protestant, especially Pentecostal, religious expansions that swept Central America in the subsequent years. The religious experience was new, as was the leadership: ordinary, often non-white, and barely lettered men using a popular language, who recall the circuit-riding preachers of 19th-century North America. The signs were there, but they slipped by most observers.

Eleven years later, I was with peasant cooperatives in the mountains of western Venezuela, where every meeting began with prayer and moved on to matters of organization and social action. In mid-1992, I joined in discussions of liberation theology in Lima, in a seminar that brought theologians, academics, activists and community leaders together to grapple with their own errors, reverses, and failures while holding to hope for the future. A few months later, at rush hour on a Friday evening, I went to the Petare station, one of the busiest Metro stops in Caracas and gateway to a large number of poor *barrios* in the east of the city. Walking into the station I found myself in the midst of a large and enthusiastic crowd: not a concert, not a political meeting, not a market, but a Pentecostal revival. There were preachers, there was music, and courteous, well-dressed young men and women circulated through the crowd inviting passersby to join them in prayer and to come to church. The atmosphere was warm and charged with energy and enthusiasm. I still remember the human warmth, the cultural effervescence, and the emotional power on display there.

I already knew intellectually about the advance of the Protestant churches, especially in poor neighborhoods. I had even, on a few occasions, heard the music, the clapping of hands, and the enthusiastic hymn-singing of the faithful praising God late into the night. But never before had I directly experienced what I felt that evening in Petare. It reminded me of scenes I had experienced elsewhere, among groups inspired by the theology of liberation: neighborhood organizations, cooperatives, women's groups, health committees, and many others. Here, as well, one encountered a sense of openness, an atmosphere of hope and cultural creativity, and the same strongly popular and working class makeup of the crowd. That night waiting for the train in Petare I remember thinking, this is really the future of religion: The future is here, in these kinds of places, in these social spaces, with ordinary men and women like this. This is where the future of religion will be built.

Encounters like these could be repeated endlessly. As discrete moments each has interest, color, and warmth. Taken together, they provide a window into the experience of change in religion, and in the place that religion claims and holds in society and politics across the region. The first point to make is that change is normal. Not long ago, this would have been a shocking statement for students of religion. Religions were assumed to be carriers of "tradition," consigned by reigning theories of secularization to privatization, decline, and disappearance. Theoretical blinders play no ideological favorites. Such views helped scholars and observers miss the religious roots of the civil rights movement in the United States just as they misread the surge of the Iranian revolution. Tocqueville's comment is apt: "Eighteenth-century philosophers had a very simple explanation for the general weakening of beliefs. Religious zeal, they said, was bound to die down as enlightenment and freedom spread. It is tiresome that the facts to do not fit this theory at all."[1]

It is not easy to see things as they are; and harder still to identify trends that are just taking form. Academics and the theories that guide them commonly play catch-up with change. Our views of the world and unstated assumptions about how things work make it easy to miss the sources and the growing evidence of change. The repeated pressure of events that run counter to expectations slowly brings scholars to abandon old theories and slowly to accept that what they see in the news is no short term aberration, but rather the leading edge of something new. Religion gives us many cases in point. Beginning with the tragedy of Jonestown, spurred at home by the rise of the religious right and abroad by the surprise of the Iranian revolution, and capped off by the disasters and lies at Waco, public images of religion have changed beyond recognition. What was once vaguely comforting and familiar to Americans has become associated with conflict, extremism, danger, violence, and upheaval. One finds attention to fundamentalisms here and around the world, talk of "religious resurgence," and concerns about the "politicization of religion"—as if what we now see had never been seen before.

The story of my own encounters with religion over the years in Latin America suggests that Latin America shares and in some way leads these unsettling experiences of change. By any measure, what we take as "religion" and what we find when we encounter it almost anywhere in the region have undergone intense and repeated waves of change, often associated with great violence. The pace of change has been so rapid, and the pattern so rich and complex, that it is sometimes hard to know where to start. One useful first step is to acknowledge that there is more religion—that is, more instances and variety and accessibility of religion—than ever before. Where a typical town or neighborhood once could be safely assumed to have one church, sparsely attended at that, one now funds multiple, competing religious offerings: evangelical chapels and charismatic movements, street preachers and religious radio and television programs. A region once comfortably assumed to be totally Roman Catholic is approaching religious pluralism. There is religious innovation; and instances of what some scholars like to call "fundamentalism" are

---

[1] Alexis de Tocqueville, *Democracy in America* (Garden City, New York: Doubleday, 1969), p. 295.

everywhere. But these rarely fit expectations derived from North American experience. At the same time, the end of the cold war, the close of civil wars in Central America, and the return of much of South America to "normal politics," have taken religious issues and actors out of the spotlight and off center stage in national political life. Where churches once stood as a "voice for the voiceless" and opposed authoritarian regimes in the name of preserving human rights and promoting democracy, we now find religious actors competing for votes, patronage, and the spoils of office. Catholic "ayatollahs" are notable for their absence, red bishops a thing of past imagination.

If we take a photograph now, how can we know if the scene we shoot hides an edge of long term change? It will not be easy. The object of our attention is a moving target, difficult to keep up with, let alone to keep in focus. The pressure to pigeonhole events and label trends is at best premature, at worst counterproductive. The Peruvian theologian Gustavo Gutiérrez has a nice way of stating the point. He writes, "At present we are in the position of those trying to decide whom a newborn child resembles. Some will say the father, others the mother, some will even find that the child has this grandfather's nose or that aunt's eyes, whereas still others will be of the opinion that the child does not remind them of any family features known to them. Better to photograph the child and decide later on whom it resembles."[2]

The question has two parts: how to get a better picture and how to know what we are seeing. Several approaches suggest themselves. One is to put together a list of themes, groups, issues, or places that are starting to occupy public attention in Latin America. This is not difficult, and I will do some relevant list-making later. But it seems to me that starting here jumps the gun. To make sense of what is, it helps to know how things got this way. If we can grasp how issues move on and off the table in Latin America, it may yield insight into how what is happening now can lead to future scenarios. One important step in this process is to stop simply extrapolating from the past—that is, to stop expecting that what used to happen will happen again. A great many points that once occupied our attention are no longer on the agenda in Latin America. Let me therefore begin with a brief account of what is no longer the case, and why.

My account begins with a period when concerns over religion and politics, and writings about the "politicization" of religion, first moved to the center of attention in the study of Latin America. From this starting point, historically situated between the mid-1960s and the late 1980s, I will work back and then forward to bring us to the present.

The bedrock of any discussion of change in religion, society, and politics has to be acknowledging the disappearance of the Catholic monopoly. Latin

---

[2] Gutierrez, Gustavo, *We Drink from Our Own Wells: The Spiritual Journey of a People,* (Maryknoll, N.Y.: Orbis Books, 1984), p. 92.

America is now approaching a state of religious pluralism (among Christian groups) for the first time in its history. This religious pluralism entails not only a multiplicity of voices speaking "in the name of religion" but also a conflict for voice *within* specific religious groups. The spread of literacy and the access to mass media have diffused the tools of religious expertise into many hands. It is no longer difficult to set up a church; the sheer growth in numbers has been startling.[3] The decay of monopoly and the approach of pluralism have also brought a shift in the focus of many religious activists. There is competition for members, and demands that official subsidies (long limited to the Catholic church) now be more widely and equitably divided. Not everything is narrowly political. A wider range of religiously linked services has appeared—schools, hospitals, publications, and groups. Whether or not this adds up to the creation of a "civil society," as some would like, the difference in the fabric of everyday life, and in the options open to ordinary people, is remarkable. A story that not long ago could be told with confidence about how Catholicism supported and reflected the established order became a story in which religion (Protestant as well as Catholic) has become a source of new ideas about how to organize society and politics, and how to lead the good life. It is no exaggeration to say that many of the region's most significant movements for change would have been unthinkable without religious participation and legitimation. If we look to the "big politics" of state and governments, and trace the history of its study, it is clear that the early boom of attention to religion and politics in Latin America came with enthusiasm over "development" and the belief that religion could provide a solid floor of values, a cultural unity assumed to be essential for economic success. Pioneering work by the late Ivan Vallier argued that if religion was to help promote change, the churches had to get out of politics. Only by cutting ties to political options, and (by extension) to existing elites and social arrangements, could religion create and promote core values. This optimistic view went hand in hand with a conviction that Christian Democratic parties could be a key vehicle for change.[4] Vallier inspired a generation of students (myself included) to take a fresh look at religion and politics, but he turned out to be wrong about the general issues and about Christian Democracy in particular. The kind of developmental project he anticipated foundered in the late 1960s as democracies collapsed across the region, Christian Democratic parties divided, and the churches themselves faced a new wave of demands to get into politics, but now to promote not development but liberation.

The origins, extensions, and impacts of liberation theology have generated a huge literature and this is not the place for a thorough review. Here it

---

[3] See David Stoll, *Is Latin America Turning Protestant? The Politics of Evangelical Growth* (Berkeley: University of California Press, 1990), ch. 6.

[4] See Ivan Vallier, *Catholicism, Social Control and Modernization in Latin America* (Englewood: Prentice Hall, 1970).

suffices to underscore that for many students and observers of the region, the energizing effects of liberation theology, which included calls for political action and opposition to states and elites, represented a case in point of the politicization of religion and a model that still provides some with a road map for tracing events. From the late 1960s to the mid-1980s, religious voices throughout Latin America outlined a radical critique of the established order of things, argued for (and helped create) a place for the poor and powerless in national life, and sparked a broad range of social innovations, including social movements.

At times it seemed as if changes arising in religion were going to spark a whole new era of cultural and political transformation. Religion began to change, and in changing seemed to be creating a foundation for major transformations of culture, society and politics. Once the reliable ally of domination, religion became a source and inspiration for freedom. New ideas about justice, rights, legitimacy, and active citizenship were put on the continent's agenda. New social movements were spawned, political alliances reconfigured, and innovative connections with politics at all levels were set in motion. This is what is often referred to as "the popular church." Ordinary people acquired confidence and skills that spilled over to reshape their views of established institutions, and remake their dealings with the world of power, politics, and privilege. Organizations were created, activists trained, martyrs produced.

The evolution of events in Central America gave this aspect of politics special prominence but Central America was never representative of the larger reality. Excessive focus on Central America skewed our perception of reality by tying the validity of the liberationist project too closely to the fortunes of political groups and movements, and exaggerating the extent of the popular involvement and support they enjoyed. The tide began to turn in the mid-1980s. Intense and effective repression took a toll, as did competition from other movements, including new churches bearing a very different political message. Allies and connections in the churches and in political parties were lost, just as major shifts in economic and political conditions made collective action substantially harder. Strong Vatican opposition, the fall of socialism in Europe, the defeat of the Sandinista regime in Nicaragua, and the growth and spread of evangelical Protestantism have reinforced a sense that the promise of liberation theology is at best played out, at worst an illusion that never was. But even if the demise of liberation theology were complete, this would not make religion and politics irrelevant to one another. The relationship continues, but the actors, issues, arenas, and ideological direction of the struggles have all been transformed.

The preceding discussion brings me to the point where we can begin specifying what is no longer the case in politics. The most obvious change comes with the involvement of religion in conflict, war, and peace. A more traditional way to put this would be to talk about church-state conflict and its links to politics more broadly defined. But however the relationship is phrased, the point remains the same: how and to what extent religious groups, activists, leaders, symbols, and resources are tied up with parties in conflict, or with the resolution of the often armed conflict. Popular imagery of religion stoking revolution—of red bishops leading the charge against governments or of an Iranian-style revolution brewing in the western hemisphere—were all the products of a fevered right wing imagination. This is not to say that there was no involvement of religion with this kind of politics. Here again, Central American experience took the lead, and nowhere more than in Guatemala, where the early growth of fundamentalist Protestantism was closely linked to the North American religious right. But there, as elsewhere, the decline of the cold war has weakened those ties and Latin American Protestants, left to their own devices, have produced a much more varied set of positions than Pat Robertson or Jerry Falwell imagined when they embraced Chile's General Pinochet or Guatemala's General Rios Montt in the 1980s.

More common was the role of churches and church-related organizations in protecting individuals or groups and servicing needs of all kind with food and shelter, legal assistance, organizational sponsorship, help with finding missing relatives, resisting torture, and caring for the victims of war, including orphans. Cases in point include Chile's justly famous Vicariate of Solidarity and Brazil's Pastoral Land Commission, along with a host of lesser known efforts by *Socorro Jurídico* in El Salvador, Quakers and groups like Witness for Peace in Nicaragua, and SERPAJ in Argentina. More recently, in the endgame of authoritarian regimes across the region, churches have played a central part in fact finding and truth commissions. This assumption of the role of "honest broker" reflects a subtle shift away from partisanship to recognizing the legitimacy of all sides, and using the extensive religious networks to promote peace. In this regard, the experience of Latin America has much in common with that of Zimbabwe and South Africa after apartheid, and with certain aspects of the fall of communism in Eastern Europe. The decline of physical violence associated with religion, has not, of course, brought a decline of violence per se. In the post-liberation environment, churches of all kinds, especially in the cities, face a kind of violence for which the ideas of liberation theology left them ill prepared. The spread of drugs and the epidemic of gang violence common to major cities of the region have thus far not met with a coherent response from the churches.[5] (See Berryman, 1996.) The same is true for family violence, which remains one of the open secrets of ordinary life.

A feature of religious life in Latin America that is worthy of note is the relative absence of millenarian or end of the world movements so notable in recent western experience. The region has seen no new prophets, no creators

[5] See Phillip Berryman, *Religion in the Megacity: Catholic and Protestant Portraits from Latin America* (Maryknoll, N.Y.: Orbis Books, 1996).

of a new Jerusalem, no armed movement that withdraws from "the world" to prepare for and await its end. Although I can think of separatist movements akin to the Branch Davidians (the Israelitas in Peru, for example) since the great Canudos Rebellion of the 19th century in Brazil, there has been no outburst of state violence against a separatist religious movement.

Just as political alignments and coalitions of a certain kind no longer hold, the pattern of public space, and its religious uses, which stood for centuries has also begun to change. The very concept of "public"—of what constitutes "public space" and who can use it—is complex. The proliferation of organizations of all kinds has helped put issues once relegated to "private" life into the public sphere, and to accustom people (especially women) to think about public solutions to private problems. These include such basic matters as water, housing, healthcare, and childcare. Although, as we shall see, many of these new organizations fail, the disposition to organize remains, and the ties between public and private continue to be reworked, even in the absence of long-lasting group structure. (See Romero.) There has also been a boom in the public spaces available for religion: new churches, chapels, and other venues where religious messages are transmitted. The latter include street corners, television stations, and public transport. Note that the proliferation and redefinition of space has been a product of the occupation of public space by new actors—men and women who hitherto had no voice, or at least were told that they had none. Although the phenomenon is visible everywhere, I limit myself here to revivals, television, and new churches.

Revivals as such and their use as a kind of technique mixing political and other messages with great emotive power before mass audiences is now common in places otherwise as distinct as Puerto Rico, Peru, Brazil, and Venezuela. Nor are revivals limited to stadiums and street corners. Latin America is a television-soaked culture area: Television programs are widely available and religious broadcasting has expanded to fill the newly available space. In some regards this is just a natural extension of radio, which has long since been developed and used by missionaries. The difference now is in the scale of the effort and in the target. Missionaries now work big cities and core population groups, not just outlying and marginal populations.

The early wave of revivals in the region had close ties with North American fundamentalism and shared in its strongly anticommunist and antileftist message. For reasons indicated earlier, those ties have weakened, and most current revivals eschew broad political goals, although they may get involved in specific issues, such as the constitutional reforms in Puerto Rico. The point is less their political affiliation than their power to move and mobilize. This was brought home to me in a visit I made to Cuba in mid-1998, as part of a delegation sponsored by the Latin American Studies Association. We went to attend a conference on society and religion, and in general to test the waters in the aftermath of Pope John Paul II's visit to the island. Alongside statements of greater openness to religion, and a clear growth of spin-off religious groups (such as the Martin Luther King Center in Havana), we encountered strong official resistance to the very idea of evangelical-style revivals or organizations, much less revivals in Cuba itself. As the experience of Falun Gong in China suggests, a group that can mobilize on that scale is a threat best kept off the stage.

The proliferation of new churches has been remarkable. Many of these are small and short-lived. In his study of the war in Guatemala's Ixil country, David Stoll shows how Protestant churches in the town of Nebaj grew from two in 1970 to 21 in 1989. For the whole *municipio* (town and surrounding hamlets), the new total was over 90. These were all small churches, generally split-offs from other Protestant start ups, founded by men with little schooling.[6] But not all new churches are small, and some are immense. Brazil has some of the world's largest independent Protestant churches, including several that are wholly autonomous foundations. The Church of the Universal Reign of God is a case in point. Founded in 1975 by Edir Macedo, the Universal Church is now a multinational institution, controlling one of Brazil's most extensive nets of mass media, including television. Its doctrine is a variant on the classic North American "prosperity theology"—the "name it and claim it" school made famous by Jim and Tammy Faye Bakker's failed PTL Ministry.

An interesting aspect of the new uses and claimants to public space is the situation of religious political parties. Explicitly confessional parties have never had much success in Latin America. Traditional Catholics identified with straight conservative movements, and beginning in the 1950s and 60s Christian Democratic parties, inspired by Catholic social doctrine but formally independent of the church, claimed religious legitimacy for their reformist agenda. These parties only attained power in Chile and Venezuela, and the Venezuelan party has now effectively disappeared as a major political force. In any event, the surge of leftist Catholic politics, embodied in liberation theology, put other claims to religious legitimacy on the table, and along with pressures from the right, left Christian Democracy divided.

But religious political activism, and explicitly religious political parties and candidates, are now enjoying something of a comeback—this time associated with Protestants and evangelical groups. Early insistence that such groups were nonpolitical confused the language of otherworldliness and personal salvation with day-to-day realities of involvement in community and national affairs. The vocal Protestant affiliation of Guatemala's General Efraín Rios Montt attracted much attention, particularly after he unleashed what was in effect a war on grassroots Catholic activists during his short but violent time in

---

[6]   Stoll, David, *Between Two Armies: In the Ixil Towns of Guatemala* (Berkeley: University of California Press, 1994).

office. Rios Montt was not Latin America's first Protestant President: That honor goes to Brazil. Nor was he the last Guatemalan Protestant to achieve high office. Jorge Elías Serrano came later, and was ousted in a sea of corruption scandals that tarnished the believers' reputation for probity.

Since these spectacular experiences, Latin American Protestant activists have slowly created a different path. The tone of Protestant voices and the direction of their political involvement have changed substantially over the years. The 1970s and 1980s were dominated by aggressive evangelism, a focus on building networks of churches and leaders for the future, and a strident anti-leftism. The salience of this agenda was reinforced by links with North American fundamentalist Protestant groups, whose involvement was mediated and enhanced by common commitments in the Central American civil wars. The end of these conflicts and the demise of Chile's Pinochet (long a favorite of the North American religious right) lowered the temperature and reduced pressure on evangelical groups to take sides in the wars or their ideological surrogates.

Around the same time, the groups and networks crafted in preceding years began to flex their muscles, reaching out for broader political influence. Evangelical churches began to press claims on the government for benefits long accorded automatically to Catholic churches and institutions. These included support for schools and for the construction and repair of church facilities. They also began to claim a place in public life as legitimate spokesmen for religion, as moral voices to be consulted, respected, and put on view equally with Catholics. This is part of a more general demand for formal recognition by the state—a demand that is as much symbolic (sharing space on public platforms) as it is material. They built alliances with social and political groups at all levels and began to construct political movements. The apparent fluke of Rios Montt's aggressively evangelical regime Guatemala was followed not much later by the free election of Jorge Elías Serrano (an evangelical candidate closely linked with Rios Montt) to the country's presidency. Soon after, Alberto Fujimori won Peru's presidency with strategic and highly visible backing from the country's Evangelical Alliance. Evangelicals aligned themselves with emerging political figures (including, most recently, Venezuela's Hugo Chavez), and at the same time organized and ran slates of explicitly evangelical candidates for public office all across the region.

Democracy was long suspect in the eyes of Catholic church leaders, but by the mid-1960s a combination of influences from European thinkers like Jacques Maritain and the Second Vatican Council, and pressures from within the ranks of the Latin American churches themselves, made democracy ideologically acceptable. This change came just as the presence of the state, once bitterly contested in areas like education, became more and more taken as a given, something to be worked with. Religion's (that is to say, the institutional Catholic church's) relation to democracy in this period is one of growing support, with confidence in development and in the capacity of middle class moderate politics to manage the process. The collapse of the region's democracies in the 1970s undermined this confidence. Although the political stances associated with liberation theology are often caricatured as a kind of simple minded revolutionary Marxism, it is fair to say that equality and change were more important to its view of the world than were democracy, elections, and competition. The slow and difficult transition back to democracy in the 1980s, and the failure of the Sandinistas to retain popular support in Nicaragua, spurred another change, and a reconsideration of democratic politics not only as inevitable, but also as good.

But there are ironies here. Central among them is that most of the affiliations and movements that arose around or were inspired by liberation theology failed to make the transition to democracy. To put it bluntly, they flourished in war and under repression but divided and disappeared in more open circumstances. The neighborhood associations, women's groups, soup kitchens, and even the human rights groups that flourished as recently as 10 or 15 years ago are no longer to be found. The popular movement that once seemed so promising as a source of new politics is gone. Why? There are some short-term reasons, including the very toll of struggle. By the early 1990s, many groups had burned out. The struggle had been exhausting; members had been killed or had simply drifted away; leaders had not been replaced; and severe economic decline meant that for numbers of grass roots followers, the struggle to survive took precedence over the political struggle. Political alliances also proved fragile. Those who placed their hopes in the Left more often than not ended up abandoned—victims of disputes that had nothing to do with their own concerns. The advent of a new conservative generation of church leadership also took a toll.

The issues have a different reality for elites and the institutions they direct than for grassroots activists and group members. Elites and institutions face the challenge of maintaining a critical presence in a very different political arena. Religious spokesmen no longer command immediate attention. Religious discourse no longer occupies center stage and even if it did, there is no longer a single voice. Activists and especially grassroots members face a more elemental challenge: how to hold members and keep organizations alive in the teeth of hard times and a state that is at best indifferent. By now it is clear that early hopes for a new politics will not be fulfilled. Everywhere in Latin America, transitions to democracy have been accompanied by demobilization and marginalization of popular movements. It is easier to hold groups together against a common enemy like the military than to choose among competing parties in an election.

The fact that political opening came accompanied by economic crisis and cuts in government structures and services put a premium on the presence of leaders and the availability of existing church and church-related networks. Activists experienced at reaching across class lines to mobilize and deliver services assumed new prominence. In many cases, grassroots groups were supplemented and even replaced by non-governmental organizations (NGOs) that often had important transnational connections. The number and variety of NGOs active in Latin America has expanded greatly over the last decade. The variety is astonishing: human rights organizations, Catholic religious orders, missionary societies, Protestant churches of all kinds, relief organizations and development agencies; research and educational foundations; environmental groups; and special purpose efforts directed at, for example, rural or urban trade unions, housing, and children. Groups like these organized throughout the region to make plans, broker resources, and provide services ranging from education, surplus food, health services, and agricultural extension to legal advice, cooperatives, and housing projects.

Although only a few of the groups in question are explicitly religious in origin and sponsorship, many have clear links with religious groups. They share ideas, agendas, personnel, and resources. Much of the staffing for such efforts comes from the ranks of the ex-clergy. It is not that churches or religiously linked groups "stepped into the breach." What happened is better described as the widening of existing gaps, the weakening of state agencies, and the disappearance of other groups, leaving these organizations with fewer competitors.

In the recent experience of activist religion in Latin America, gender issues have played a critical role. Women comprised the vast majority of the membership of grass roots religious groups. This had less to do with the supposedly greater piety of women than with the appeal of religiously sanctioned organizations to people for whom organization and activity outside the home was something new. Women quickly took the opportunities and became active in new ways across the region. Because church organizations were culturally sanctioned vehicles for women, they drew hitherto silent voices into public spaces. But many women remained wary of specifically political activism and constrained by family obligations—including pressure from male relatives to stay out of politics, which is seen as "men's work." All this shaped the kind of activism that most group members were disposed to support. They would commit themselves with enthusiasm and bravery to local issues but resist recruitment for broader agendas. They would filter out activist and conflict-centered messages. The result was that they followed leaders only so far, but no further. The choices were difficult, and often led to ultimate abandonment of activism[7] (Drogus 1997a, 1997b).

The preceding observations raise some obvious questions: What has hap-

---

[7] See C. Drogus, "Private Power or Public Power Pentecostalism, Base Communities and Gender" in Edward L. Cleary and Hannah Stewart-Gambino, eds., *Power, Politics and Pentecostals in Latin America* (Boulder, Col.: Westview Press, 1997), pp. 55-75; and C. Drogus, *Women, Religion, and Social Change in Brazil's Popular Church* (South Bend: University of Notre Dame Press, 1997).

pened to the activists? What has happened to activism as a general disposition? What is the fate of all those mobilizing energies, all those organizational skills? There is no clear answer yet, but there are some indications. Let us be clear that nothing is unusual about the problems of Latin America's religiously inspired movements. Most social movements in most places fail. Heroic activism is difficult to sustain in the best of circumstances. The more common experience is a cycle of protest in which activists recognize a crack in existing systems of social and political control, movements proliferate, and then they decay. In any event, it seems clear that participation and activism can be compartmentalized, such that skills can be put to use in local and community events without this necessarily feeding into a larger organizational net. These efforts are no less genuine for being limited in scope. I suggest, therefore, that we look at the local level, and at less explicitly political spaces, to get a sense of the kinds of interests and energies brewing "out there." This means looking to churches, schools, local and perhaps regional networks, and to a range of issues more commonly considered private than public. The yield will be organizations that come and go according to the issues. It is also worth recognizing that action is costly, especially for ordinary people who operate on the slimmest of margins. This suggests that rather than replacing older attitudes of submission or pleading, activism may be seen by many as an alternative, useful as far as it goes. Activism may also be more likely in bursts, in efforts that fill a suddenly visible gap, rather than in sustained campaigns.

It is important to say a few words about fundamentalism—but only a few. Writing about fundamentalism has been a growth industry in recent years, to the point that any religious activism or militancy is commonly labeled "fundamentalist" and the term has lost its meaning. In the case of Latin America, the undoubted growth and expansion of Protestant churches of all kinds has drawn attention to the prospects of fundamentalism in the region. But everything new is not fundamentalist, nor are all fundamentalists the same. It is important to recognize distinctions within Latin American Protestantism, and in particular to distinguish Pentecostal churches from their fundamentalist cousins. As in the United States, the former are much less drawn into political alliances than the latter. I am reminded of a comment by Nancy Ammerman, a distinguished student of religion in contemporary North America (including fundamentalism), to the effect that "fundamentalists tie their shoes." The implication is that those we call fundamentalists are not aliens, inexplicably caught up in some weird doctrine. Nor do they spend all, or even most of their time in "militancy." They also tie their shoes, raise and school their children, construct communities, and make (they hope) a living.

A striking feature of Protestantism, including the fundamentalist variety, in Latin America has been its consistent appeal to both sexes. The common wisdom holds that fundamentalism is, well, fundamentally patriarchal, and thus reinforces male domination in family, society, and politics. There is considerable truth in this, but recent research affirms both its powerful appeal to women and an impact on men that reins in and controls male prerogative while at the same time supporting male domination. The two are related. The appeal to women has much to do with the vision of a stable family life in which drunkenness and serial monogamy are banned. The appeal to men, in contrast, is often linked to a sense of crisis overcome—be the crisis drunkenness, unemployment, migration, loneliness, or homelessness. Attention to the preaching and recruitment of these churches will uncover less politics and more healing, less activism and more spiritual crisis, than their common image conveys. The political fallout is mixed and sometimes curious. For example, neighborhood cleanups and the construction of local church-linked businesses to combat the effects of economic crisis dramatically reinforce traditional Catholic anti-pornography and censorship campaigns.

In thinking about the future and how to see it coming, we must at once think about politics in different ways and expand our horizons beyond politics, however politics ends up being defined. If we have learned anything at all from the experience of religion in the public sphere in recent years, it is surely that the boundaries of the political have been pushed outwards. Politics is no longer the exclusive preserve of governments; all kinds of local and seemingly uncoordinated actions can constitute politics. But by the same token, the new politics created here may not lend itself well to the construction of movements and organizations. Perhaps its strength lies in the mobilization of opinion, of a civil society that in many senses was not there before. It also helps if we think about religion's encounter with politics and democracy in Latin America less as a linear trajectory, moving inexorably from one point to another, than as a cycle. As cycles of protest rise, organizational innovations are tried out, new paths are opened for political and social action, and members of hitherto marginal groups are drawn into action. After a while, opposition grows and opponents find ways to counter the initial surge, activists tire, conditions change. This should be no surprise.

When we look beyond politics, we find a terrain that is rich with change. The religious transformations sketched out here have the potential to set in motion long-term changes in culture and social life. Take the relations between the sexes. Gender relations are notoriously slow to change and famously resistant to pressure from institutions. It is worth thinking that a less directed process of change in gender relations and family life may be underway in the region. By stressing stable families and reining in male sexuality, the new generation of Protestant churches has an edge on transforming a central aspect of every day life. The Catholic Church has been slow to acknowledge gender issues as legitimate. Problems specific to women—including spousal abuse, sexual harassment, and limited access to jobs or schooling—are folded into a general critique of exploitation with roots in class inequalities. Liberationist discourse and the organizations that rely on it promote a "unisex" standard emphasizing female participation in the public sphere. As noted earlier, this has had limited success.

Despite the unquestioned expansion of Protestant churches, in most countries the Roman Catholic Church remains dominant, and for many continues to be "the church." An unanswered question for the future of religion in Latin America hinges on the future of changes within the Catholic Church generally. There is likely to be a change in the papacy in the next few years, but regardless of what directions Vatican policy takes, it seems clear that the groundwork has been laid for a long run of conservative leadership in the Catholic churches of the region. For almost 20 years now, Vatican policy has been to replace liberationist bishops with those more sympathetic to papal views, purge seminaries and publishing houses, and restrain excessively independent "politicized" groups. There can be no question that this has had an effect. One area to look at, then, is the current status of regional Catholic institutions, such as the conferences of bishops and religious orders. Although their days of actively promoting social and political change seem well past, this does not rule out the taking of public stands on a wide range of issues, from ecology and land use to housing and unemployment.

The Catholic Church no longer holds a monopoly on the creation and use of continent-wide religious organizations. The proliferation of religious NGOs, from the transnational to the locally based, range from confederations of churches to networks of publishing houses and school associations. There are now two competing Protestant organizations: the Latin American Council of Churches (CLAI, or Conferencia LatinoAmericana de Iglesias), which groups the more historical and liberationist churches and has ties to the World Council of Churches), and the Latin American Evangelical Fellowship, comprised of more evangelical groups. Neither of these organizations can contain the mushrooming and typically fissiparous Pentecostal churches. Organizations of this kind are a fascinating mix of clearing house and training ground. As they grow and become more institutionalized, they are likely to be an important source of new positions and initiatives, brokering ideas and resources.

In the 1980s, religion was pushed and pulled onto center stage by a powerful combination of new ideas, effective leaders, and populations eager to make sense of their situation and find moral sanction and allies in their search for solutions. As circumstances changed, religion not surprisingly assumed a less prominent role. But moving off center stage does not mean moving out of the public sphere. Hopes that the restoration of democracy would mean bring a thorough depoliticization of religion have already been disappointed. Why expect religion to be depoliticized in Latin America, when religious issues and groups flourish in politics all around the world, not least in the United States?

At issue is not depoliticization or abandonment of the public sphere, but rather a shift in who speaks and what exactly they say. The prime focus and level of action has also shifted.

If we ask who speaks for religion in Latin America today, the answer is not at all clear. Whereas once religion meant the Roman Catholic Church and the Roman Catholic Church meant its hierarchy, there is now a proliferation of voices and of venues for their expression. Any list of those who "speak for the Catholic Church" on social and political issues, therefore, must include (at least) the Pope; regional organizations such as CELAM (Conferencia Episcopal Latino Americana, the Latin American Bishops' Conference), and CLAR (Conferencia Latino Americana de Religiosos, the Latin American Conference of Religious Orders), which are often at odds with one another; relevant national hierarchies; individual prelates and specific religious orders; magazines and publishing houses; research institutes, universities and schools; local clergy, sisters and activists; intermediate structures such as the Vicariate of Solidarity and the Comisao Pastoral da Terra; and a host of lay-inspired and run action groups. This is not to say that there is no unity at all. The passage of time and events plus consistent Vatican pressure for a restoration of authority have molded a broadly common agenda which, if it does not go all the way in the direction Rome wants, nonetheless manages to move the center of gravity of discourse and action far from where it was at the high point of liberationist discourse in the 1970s.

The building blocks of a new agenda for the Catholic Church are these. First is a steady condemnation of violence, an avoidance wherever possible of involvement in violence, and a consistent commitment to broad definitions of human rights. Second is withdrawal in most cases from open political and partisan alliances and connections. Third, there is a shift in the locus of activism away from big structures and national issues to a patient, long-term effort directed at the creation of resources and accumulation of social capital at the local level. To be sure, directing attention to the local level without a sustained effort to build and hold membership, without energies devoted to conferences, publications, and the elaboration of organizational structures, is wasted effort. The point is that the situation and the understanding of what is at issue in building a movement has changed considerably. Movements now find fewer allies in state and political parties. They operate more and more to fill spaces left empty as the neo-liberal state has withdrawn from social intervention. They draw resources increasingly from volunteers, from a host of small scale enterprises, and not least from NGOs.

The pluralization of religious voices has immediate consequences for democracy. To begin with, in a plural environment, it is to everyone's interest to maintain open civil society with guarantees of free speech and equal access to institutions and to public spaces. The continuing erosion of Catholicism's monopoly status thus bears on a host of traditional issues from censorship and education to subsidies and representation in government commissions, committees, and public platforms. Set in the general political context, pluralization also suggests that building and sustaining a new role will require groups to play the old politics more skillfully and more consistently than in the past. This means sustaining grassroots democracy while working on allies and connections and assuming a realistic bargaining stance to politics. Continued work at the local level is the bedrock on which anything else must be built. Groups need to bargain for better terms with everyone and enter into alliances only with great care and caution. Allies, connections, resources, and the shield they provide remain of critical importance. The point to bear in mind is that, groups and collections of activists remain a vital presence, above all at the local level. They have been central to the construction of popular movements, and have energized urban politics throughout the region. Is this failure, or do we need a different measure of success?

It has become common in writings on religion and politics in Latin America to dismiss stress on continued democratization as a romantic hangover from the golden period of liberation theology: one among many illusions, another bubble to burst. But this confuses the undoubted organizational problems of liberation theology with the power that democratizing movements can have to enrich social life and create meaningful new identities. On reflection, it is clear that much of the power of liberationist ideas came from the way they held a mirror up to the prevailing order of things and its operative rules of the game: to hierarchy and equality, to state control and autonomy, to passivity and activism, to impunity, justice and accountability. Claims were advanced that are new to the culture of Latin American politics.

At the heart of these claims is a view of legitimacy and of legitimate politics grounded in elements that are new to the culture of Latin American politics: transparency, accountability, participation through organizations, and a definition of governance less wedded to order and control from above. Transparency and accountability require that official decisions be open to public scrutiny, and that officials themselves be responsible for their action: subject to the same law they impose. Enforcing these demands requires diffusing authority and multiplying points of citizen access to the political arena. Although grassroots groups cannot by themselves guarantee open and equitable politics, their creation and continuing presence, above all in local politics, is an important step in this direction. One consequence has been to place the theme of citizenship—that is, of the human and civil rights of persons—at the forefront of popular movements, avoiding the assumption of earlier radicalism that there could be no citizenship without a total transformation of society. The result may finally be effective pressure from below for that modernization of the state and of institutions of political representation that is so conspicuously lacking in the region.

The final issue I want to mention is religious competition. Earlier I under-

scored the extent to which Latin America is now approaching a situation of genuine religious pluralism. Catholicism may still be the single most powerful
force, but the Catholic Church can no longer pretend to be the only authenti-
cally religious voice in the region. The advent of pluralism has brought competition for faithful and some significant elbowing for public support and financing. Although incidents of religious strife are thus far thankfully rare, it is fair
to say that ecumenism has not been the dominant note of interchurch relations.
The Catholic hierarchy complains repeatedly about "the invasion of the sects"
and worries about the erosion of what in their eyes is Latin America's uniquely
Catholic culture. Many of the newer Protestant groups evidence open hostility
to the Catholic Church, and references to the church as "the whore of Babylon"
are not uncommon. Aided by mass communications, these conflicts have sometimes erupted on a wide scale, as in the famous case when a representative of
Brazil's Universal Church of the Kingdom of God, in a program broadcast on
the church's television network mocked an effigy of Our Lady of Aparecida,
Brazil's patron saint, and even nudged it with his foot. The episode became
known in the media as the *chute na Santa*—"shoot for saint" (*chute* being the
term for a kick, as derived from the English soccer expression "shoot for goal").
The result was a conflict waged on television and later transposed into the
courts as each group challenged the others legitimacy. The Universal Church
was accused of promoting magic, charlatanism, and improperly taking the
money of the faithful in return for promised gifts of the spirit. Legal actions
were eventually brought against the Universal Church for "crimes against religious faith," including public denigration of a religious object. The head of the
church, Edir Macedo, was referred to as no more than a *caca-niquel*, a slot
machine, taking in money in return for a promise of riches.

Most conflicts lack the high theater of this incident, but perhaps for that
very reason they deserve our close attention. Religion in Latin America has
been the scene of so much change in so little time that, to use a colloquial
expression, there is a lot of shaking out to be done. Not much is settled and all
we can be sure of is the likelihood of continued innovation, and of a religious
scene that is increasingly urban, multiple, and multi-faceted. Religious people
now seek a hearing on the streets, in small chapels, modest churches, and
cathedrals. They organize radio and television stations and run sizeable businesses. Managing religious pluralism and competition will not be easy, but it is
clearly high on this century's agenda. My lone market preacher is now many
voices. That is something really new.

Issues to Keep an Eye on

Youths and gang violence. Latin America's big cities have many of the problems of big cities everywhere, including drugs, youth violence, and gangs. The area's megalopolises (Sao Paulo, Mexico City, Lima, Caracas) are also centers of significant religious innovation and competition; it is in the cities that new churches, including Pentecostal churches, have grown the most rapidly. Seeking an audience and a recruitment base for new members, the churches must engage the overwhelmingly young and highly mobile population of the cities and address their concerns directly. Issues of youth, violence, drugs, and urban social disorder have been central to the recruitment of many expanding evangelical churches, which work hard in slums and around bus and other transport facilities, and find many recruits among the fallen. The Catholic church, tied to older institutional forms like the parish, has done less well.

Transnational groups. Although churches and religious institutions obviously cut across international borders, it is still common for questions about religion and society to be framed in terms of specific local or national societies. This makes sense for many purposes, but even a casual look at day-to-day life across Latin America reveals a growing presence of human and material resources, individuals and groups, ideas, and programs set in motion and linked together by transnational ties. For example, Salvadorans in San Salvador and Washington, and Peruvians in Lima and Los Angeles, maintain vital links between the home country and the diaspora. Churches follow the fortunes of migrants, and recruit members at both ends of the pipeline. Scholars have also followed youth gangs with branches in different countries, explored the dynamics of international economic development work, and looked at transnational human rights activism. The communicational and travel networks that accompany religious movements, both Catholic and non-Catholic, mean that there is a much greater degree of transparency in what goes on within any given country. In other words, repression and oppression cannot be carried out by governments in the informational void they once enjoyed.

Public space. Latin America's public space has been expanded in transformed in recent years by an explosion of community and neighborhood groups, private organizations and foundations, and local and regional cultural organizations. Together they constitute the basis of a new "civil society" that is more autonomous from the state than ever before. Along with the transitions to civilian rule and democratic politics that have transformed Latin America's political landscape in recent years, there has been a process of "structural adjustment" that entails at the very least an effort to reduce public deficits, scale back official bureaucracies, and privatize state-held industries while turning traditional public obligations, such as schooling and welfare, over to private hands. As state institutions have lost resources and shed responsibilities, non-governmental organizations (NGOs) of all kinds, many with religious affiliations, have taken them on. Schools and community centers have been created; rotating credit groups and cooperatives have been established; and institutions to promote transport, housing, and legal assistance have been set up. Many of these initiatives begin on a small scale, and then grow with help from religious or other institutions and with financing and advice from transnational groups. At the same time, the appearance of a new kind of civil society has been facilitated by the greater literacy and organizational skills of a more urban and educated population. They provided the impetus behind popular resistance to military rule in the 1980s. They lead the way in local and regional initiatives of all kinds.

New political role for the churches. Just as Latin America's churches had an important role in denouncing violations in human rights in the 1970s and 1980s, they now play a key part as a political actors at moments when there is a vacuum of leadership or of opposition. Almost every survey of public opinion in Latin America shows that churches are among the most respected and trusted of all institutions. For as citizens come to view corruption as a problem—and the mass media focus on it and politicians use as a weapon against other politicians—traditional parties, elites, and institutions can lose legitimacy to such an extent that the Catholic Church becomes an important political actor. This has happened in Venezuela in the past few years, and most recently the Church has engaged President Hugo Chávez in a major debate over his own incipient authoritarian tendencies. This kind of political role differs from that traditionally ascribed to churches in the region, which was to promote one candidate or another, or simply to resist communism or immorality. The new role is more of a critical, nonpartisan voice of civic virtue.

Revivals. Religious revivals are relatively new in Latin American experience, and they have proven so popular that the technique (evangelistic campaigns and big, emotion-filled public meetings) is now migrating from the Protestant into the Catholic sphere. The Catholic Charismatic Renewal (CCR) is one of the most rapidly growing movements in the area. CCR groups draw on charismatic elements including an emphasis on direct experience of the divine, and the exaltation of gifts of the spirit.

The Future of the Catholic Church. Despite the notable advances made by Protestant churches, the Catholic Church remains dominant throughout Latin America. Notwithstanding its age and image of continuity, the Catholic Church is an institution in continuous change. Change and reaction within Catholicism has been a constant of the last few decades, and will be particularly evident in the near future when a new Pope takes office, and some of the conservative and "restorationist" trends put into place by John Paul II come into full flower. A generation of young conservative bishops will be leading Catholic institutions, including purged seminaries and publishing houses, into the next decades. Allied with organizations like Opus Dei, these leaders will challenge the traditional intellectual dominance of the Jesuits. The struggle for control of Catholic schools and universities is already underway in many countries. But conservative groups do not lack for opposition. More liberal, even liberationist theologians, continue to find allies throughout the Church, and continued struggle over issues such as the independence of lay groups, the status of women, and the social and political alliances of the church, is likely to remain a central theme.

References

Berryman, Phillip. *Religion in the Megacity. Catholic and Protestant Portraits from Latin America*. Maryknoll, N.Y.: Orbis Books, 1996.

_____. *Stubborn Hope Religion, Politics and Revolution in Central America*. Maryknoll, N.Y.: The New Press—Orbis Books, 1994.

Drogus, C. "Private Power or Public Power Pentecostalism, Base Communities and Gender." *Power, Politics and Pentecostals in Latin America*. Eds. Edward L. Cleary and Hannah Stewart-Gambino. Boulder, Col.: Westview Press, 1997, pp. 55-75.

_____. *Women, Religion, and Social Change in Brazil's Popular Church*. South Bend: University of Notre Dame Press, 1997.

Freston, Paul. "Brother Votes For Brother: The New Politics of Protestantism in Brazil." *Rethinking Protestantism in Latin America*. Eds. D. Stoll and V. Garrard Burnett. Philadelphia: Temple University Press, 1993, pp. 66-110.

Gutierrez, Gustavo. *We Drink from Our Own Wells: The Spiritual Journey of a People*. Maryknoll, N.Y.: Orbis Books, 1984.

Lehmann, D., ed. "Special Issue on Social Movements and Religious Change," *Bulletin of Latin American Research* 18:2 (April, 1999).

_____. *Struggle for the Spirit: Religious Transformation and Popular Culture in Brazil and Latin America*. Oxford: Polity Press. 1996.

_____. *Democracy and Development in Latin America. Economics, Politics and Religion in the Postwar Period*. Philadelphia: Temple University Press, 1990.

Lehmann, D. and Patrician Birman. "Religion and the Media in a Battle for Ideological Hegemony: The Universal Church of the Kingdom of God and TV Globo In Brazil." *Bulletin of Latin American Research* 18:2 (1999), pp. 145-64.

Levine, Daniel H. "Revolutionaries, 'The Cause' and the Truth." *Human Rights Review* 1:1 (Oct.-Dec., 1999), pp. 98-103.

Levine, Daniel H. and D. Stoll. "Bridging the Gap Between Empowerment and Power in Latin America." *Transnational Religion and Fading States*. Eds. Suzanne H. Rudolph and J. Piscatori. Boulder, Col.: Westview Press, 1997, pp. 63-103.

_____. "On Premature Reports of the Death of Liberation Theology." *The Review of Politics* 57:1 (Winter, 1995), pp. 105-131.

_____. *Popular Voices in Latin American Catholicism*. Princeton: Princeton University Press, 1992.

_____. "How not to Understand Liberation Theology, Nicaragua or Both." *Journal of Interamerican Studies and World Affairs* 32:3 (Fall, 1990), pp. 229-45.

Martin, David. *Tongues of Fire The Explosion of Protestantism in Latin America*. Oxford: Basil Blackwell, 1990.

Pagnucco, Ronald and John D. McCarthy. "Advocating Nonviolent Direct Action in Latin America: The Antecedents and Emergence of SER-PAJ." B. Misztal and A. Shupe eds., *Religion and Politics in Comparative Perspective*. Westport, Conn.: Praeger, 1992.

Pearce, Jenny. *Promised Land: Peasant Rebellion in Chalatenango, El Salvador*. London: Latin America Bureau, 1996.

Prevot Schapira, Marie-France, "From Utopia to Pragmatism: The Heritage of *Basismo* in Local Government in the Greater Buenos Aires Region." *Bulletin of Latin American Research* 18:2 (1999), pp. 227-240.

Riviere d'Arc, Helene, "Has *Basismo* Disappeared?" *Bulletin of Latin American Research* 18:2 (April, 1999), pp. 199-211.

Smilde, David A. "Letting God Govern: Supernatural Agency in the Venezuelan Pentecostal Approach to Social Change. *Sociology of Religion* 59:3 (Fall 1998), 287-303.

Smith, Brian H. *Protestants and Catholics in Latin America*. South Bend: University of Notre Dame Press, 1998.

Stoll, David. *Between Two Armies. In the Ixil Towns of Guatemala*. New York: Columbia University Press, 1993.

_____. *Is Latin America Turning Protestant? The Politics of Evangelical Growth*. Berkeley: University of California Press, 1990.

Tocqueville, Alexis de. *Democracy in America*. Garden City, New York: Doubleday, 1969.

Vallier, Ivan. *Catholicism, Social Control and Modernization in Latin America*. Englewood Cliffs, N.J.: Prentice Hall, 1970.

Waliggo, J. M. The Role of Christian Churches in the Democratisation Process in Uganda 1980-1993. In *The Christian Churches and the Democratisation of Africa*, edited by P. Gifford. Leiden: E. J. Brill, 1995.

Williams, Pat and Toyin Falola. *Religious Impact on the Nation State*. Aldershot, U.K.: Avebury, 1995.

The Leonard E. Greenberg Center for the Study of Religion in Public Life was established at Trinity College in 1996 to advance knowledge and understanding of the varied roles that religious movements, institutions, and ideas play in the contemporary world; to explore challenges posed by religious pluralism and tensions between religious and secular values; and to examine the influence of religion on politics, culture, family life, gender roles, and other issues in the United States and elsewhere in the world.

Nonsectarian and nonpartisan, the Center sponsors public lectures, organizes conferences and workshops, contributes to the liberal arts curriculum, and supports the publication and dissemination of materials for both academic and general audiences.

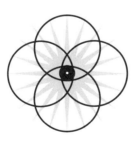

*The Leonard E. Greenberg Center is
supported by the Pew Charitable Trusts
and the Lilly Endowment, and with funds from
Leonard E. Greenberg and the Leonard E. Greenberg Endowment
for Judaic and Middle Eastern Studies at Trinity College.*

Religion on the International News Agenda

is published by

THE PEW PROGRAM ON RELIGION AND THE NEWS MEDIA

THE LEONARD E. GREENBERG CENTER
FOR THE STUDY OF RELIGION IN PUBLIC LIFE

Trinity College

300 Summit Street

Hartford, CT 06106

For copies of this book or further information

about the Center and its programs,

please contact the Center at

(860) 297-2353 or FAX (860) 297-5125

Electronic mail: **csrpl@trincoll.edu**

A complete archive of Center publications is available online at

Web site: **http://www.trincoll.edu/depts/csrpl/** Default.htm

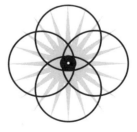